Digital leaders and business analysts must carefully evaluate whether to build or buy components for their digital solutions. *Defining Digital Solutions* offers clear, practical insights to guide this decision while ensuring business alignment.

Joris Schut CISA CBAB CGEIT, *Business Advisor, BearingPoint*

Defining Digital Solutions is a great guide to how digital products are created. It explains the key steps before development begins. A valuable guide for business analysts, architects, technologists, or anyone involved in building digital solutions.

Sibasis Padhi, *Senior Software Engineer, Walmart Associates Inc.*

A comprehensive and thought-provoking introduction to a wide range of themes and topics, which when considered together will lead to the successful definition of a robust and holistic digital solution. A fine piece of work.

Paul Turner FBCS, *BCS author and ex-Chief Examiner for the Diploma in Solution Development*

Comprehensive and well-written, I wish this guide to the various roles, tools and techniques involved in defining digital solutions had existed when I started my IT career over 25 years ago.

David Smith CITP MBCS MIET, *Customer Journey Manager, Lloyds Banking Group*

It is a one-stop shop for diving into the world of digital solutions from the perspective of an IT Business Analyst. I wish I had it when I started my career!

Iurii Gomon, *Founder, The Passionate Business Analyst*

A comprehensive and well-articulated reference book for anyone navigating the complexity of IT change delivery. It will set early career professionals on the right tracks whilst providing food for thought to seasoned experts.

Virginie Terry, *Business Analyst Manager, RSA Insurance, part of the Intact Group*

Defining Digital Solutions is a comprehensive guide to digital solutions, covering system modelling, backlog management and tools, essential for decision-makers and IT specialists. A well-defined digital solution is not just a product; it is a bridge between business needs and technological innovation

Boby Jose, *Senior Test Manager, Sogeti UK, part of Capgemini and the author of BCS book 'Test Automation'*

Gain an in-depth knowledge of the diverse range of digital solutions and development frameworks. This book emphasises the importance of aligning digital solutions with business objectives to ensure effective organisational advancement.

Rizwana Qureshi, *Customer Journey Lead, Lloyds Banking Group PLC*

DEFINING DIGITAL SOLUTIONS

BCS, THE CHARTERED INSTITUTE FOR IT

BCS, The Chartered Institute for IT, is committed to making IT good for society. We use the power of our network to bring about positive, tangible change. We champion the global IT profession and the interests of individuals, engaged in that profession, for the benefit of all.

Exchanging IT expertise and knowledge
The Institute fosters links between experts from industry, academia and business to promote new thinking, education and knowledge sharing.

Supporting practitioners
Through continuing professional development and a series of respected IT qualifications, the Institute seeks to promote professional practice tuned to the demands of business. It provides practical support and information services to its members and volunteer communities around the world.

Setting standards and frameworks
The Institute collaborates with government, industry and relevant bodies to establish good working practices, codes of conduct, skills frameworks and common standards. It also offers a range of consultancy services to employers to help them adopt best practice.

Become a member
Over 70,000 people including students, teachers, professionals and practitioners enjoy the benefits of BCS membership. These include access to an international community, invitations to a roster of local and national events, career development tools and a quarterly thought-leadership magazine. Visit www.bcs.org to find out more.

Further information
BCS, The Chartered Institute for IT,
3 Newbridge Square,
Swindon, SN1 1BY, United Kingdom.
T +44 (0) 1793 417 417
(Monday to Friday, 09:00 to 17:00 UK time)
www.bcs.org/contact

shop.bcs.org/
publishing@bcs.uk

bcs.org/qualifications-and-certifications/certifications-for-professionals/

DEFINING DIGITAL SOLUTIONS

Peter Thompson

Published by BCS Learning and Development Ltd, a wholly owned subsidiary of BCS, The Chartered Institute for IT, 3 Newbridge Square, Swindon, SN1 1BY, UK.
www.bcs.org

EU GPSR Authorised Representative: LOGOS EUROPE, 9 rue Nicolas Poussin, 17000, La Rochelle, France.
Email: Contact@logoseurope.eu

Paperback ISBN: 978-1-78017-7052
PDF ISBN: 978-1-78017-7069
ePUB ISBN: 978-1-78017-7076

British Cataloguing in Publication Data.
A CIP catalogue record for this book is available at the British Library.

Publisher's acknowledgements
Reviewers: Holly Cummins, Amanda Chessell, Catherine Plumridge, Maria Papastashi
Publisher: Ian Borthwick
Commissioning editor: Heather Wood
Production manager: Florence Leroy
Project manager: Sunrise Setting Ltd
Copy-editor: Gary Smith
Proofreader: Barbara Eastman
Indexer: David Gaskell
Cover design: Alex Wright
Cover image: istock/Nikolay Pandev
Sales director: Charles Rumball
Typeset by Lapiz Digital Services, Chennai, India

CONTENTS

LIST OF FIGURES AND TABLES

ABOUT THE AUTHOR

Peter Thompson, having graduated from Leicester Polytechnic (now De Montfort University) in 1988 with a bachelor's degree in computer science, has amassed over 35 years' experience working in a variety of business change and solution development roles, including junior programmer, project manager, information systems consultant, systems development manager and managing director of an independent software house. His experience spans a diverse range of industries working with clients from broadcasting, utilities, logistics, financial services, commodities trading, food service, recruitment and leisure hire.

A Fellow of BCS, The Chartered Institute for IT, Peter is currently Learning Services Director at Assist Knowledge Development Ltd, an external examiner for the BCS International Diploma in Business Analysis, chief examiner for the BCS International Diploma in Solution Development and a member of the Leadership Panel for the BCS Business Systems Development certification schemes. He specialises in best practice techniques and standards in business analysis, data analysis and Agile software development, subjects that he continues to teach and practise today.

FOREWORD

Technology is a core and vital driver of business change and an enabler of effective business service delivery. Well-defined digital solutions underpin the work conducted by organisations, enabling them to achieve their strategic objectives by operating efficiently and offering the required support to their customers. However, poor digital solutions have the opposite effect and risk exposing an organisation's vulnerabilities and unsatisfactory work practices.

Digital solution development is complex and requires contributions from the many distinct professions working within the digital transformation industry, each of which offers extensive knowledge and skill. However, the range of digital transformation roles has proliferated over recent years, increasing the possibility for change professionals to work in a fragmented way. This has resulted in reduced awareness of the holistic context, in particular the need to focus on achieving desired business outcomes, understand the end-to-end digital solution development process and respond to the issues and concerns that inevitably arise. Given this context, this book offers the much-needed information and guidance that will aid all digital transformation professionals.

The need to investigate a situation, identify and evaluate the available options, and define the desired solution is paramount when developing a digital solution. Rushing into the development process risks delivering a digital solution that fails to meet the organisation's needs and undermines each delivered service and value proposition. Yet, in many situations, organisations purchase, licence or develop digital products without considering their relevance to the context and the customer experience they are required to support. *Defining Digital Solutions* addresses this issue, emphasising that the process has to begin by understanding the problem a solution will resolve and clarifying the requirements it should fulfil.

Digital solutions may be developed or acquired in a number of different ways and there are numerous factors involved in deciding exactly how this will be achieved. Knowledge and understanding of the approaches applied during the development process, and their advantages and disadvantages, is essential if digital solution professionals are to ensure their contribution is effective and supports the delivery of a solution that meets the organisation's requirements.

Defining Digital Solutions provides a comprehensive explanation of the frameworks, principles and techniques that all digital transformation professionals should understand. It offers readers advice on how to navigate the key standards applied when defining digital solutions, helping them to appreciate the different specialist areas and conduct their work effectively.

The clear examples and figures provided in this book bring to life the information provided, enhancing the learning offered. The guidance provided is extensive, enabling digital transformation professionals, and those in related disciplines, to understand the breadth of knowledge they require to conduct their work effectively, navigate the complexities inherent in digital solution definition and collaborate effectively with a range of fellow professionals and business stakeholders.

Dr Debra Paul
CEO, AssistKD

ACKNOWLEDGEMENTS

As is the case with many books, this book owes its existence to many individuals who have helped shape the final product.

First, I must extend a special thanks to James Cadle, who conceived, co-authored and edited the predecessor of this series (*Developing Information Systems: Practical Guidance for IT Professionals*). Without his early support and contribution this book would not have been possible.

I would also like to extend my gratitude to my wife, Sue, whose patience during many long hours of writing during evenings, weekends and holidays is laudable. I would also like to thank my step-daughter, Sophie, for her encouragement and support throughout this project, and special thanks to my son, Alex Bradley-Thompson, who contributed his extensive knowledge of data analytics and business intelligence to Book 2 of this series, as well as acting as a sounding board and generally being there to empathise with the challenges of long hours writing and rewriting.

My colleagues at AssistKD have been hugely supportive during the writing of this book, and have contributed through many discussions on a variety of topics. In particular, Debra Paul (who also kindly provided the Foreword), Julian Cox and Fraser Morris, who have meticulously reviewed various chapters and provided incredibly helpful feedback, and Megan Sullivan, who has produced some great images to illustrate some of the chapters of Books 2 and 3 in the series.

Finally, this book could not have been produced without the professional publishing know-how of Ian Borthwick and Heather Wood from BCS – their patience and flexibility as numerous deadlines have been pushed back due to other work commitments is exemplary. I have benefited greatly from their expert advice.

ABBREVIATIONS

AI	artificial intelligence
API	application programming interface
AWS	Amazon Web Services
BA	business analyst
BASF	Business Analysis Service Framework
BCLC	business change life cycle
BDD	behaviour-driven development
BI	business intelligence
BPMN	Business Process Model and Notation
BRD	Business Requirements Document
CARE	computer-aided requirements engineering
CASE	computer-aided software engineering
CD	continuous delivery/continuous deployment
CI	continuous integration
CM	configuration management
COTS	commercial off-the-shelf
CRM	customer relationship management
CSF	critical success factor
DBMS	database management system
DoD	definition of done
DoR	definition of ready
DSDM	Dynamic Systems Development Method
EA	enterprise architecture
ERD	entity-relationship diagram
ERP	enterprise resource planning
ESG	environmental, social and governance
GDPR	General Data Protection Regulation
IaaS	infrastructure as a service
IAM	identity and access management
IDE	integrated development environment

INVEST	independent, negotiable, valuable, estimable, small, testable
IoT	Internet of Things
IP	intellectual property
IT	information technology
LSD	Lean Software Development
MDA	Model-Driven Architecture
MOTS	modified off-the-shelf
MVC	model view controller
MVP	minimum viable product
MVVM	model view viewmodel
OO	object-oriented
OPOPOT	one person, one place, one time
PaaS	platform as a service
PID	Project Initiation Document
PM	project manager
PO	product owner
POPIT	People, Organisation, Processes, Information and Technology
QA	quality assurance
RAD	Rapid Application Development
RE	Requirements Engineering
ROI	return on investment
RPA	robotic process automation
SaaS	software as a service
SDLC	software development life cycle
SEO	search engine optimisation
SLA	service level agreement
SME	subject-matter expert
SysML	Systems Modeling Language
TCO	total cost of ownership
TDD	test-driven development
ToR	terms of reference
UAT	user acceptance testing
UI	user interface
UML	Unified Modeling Language
UX	user experience
WIP	work in progress
WSJF	Weighted Shortest Job First
XP	Extreme Programming

PREFACE

In today's rapidly evolving digital landscape, organisations face unprecedented challenges and opportunities. Technology is no longer just a support function – it is a strategic enabler, driving innovation, improving efficiency and creating new avenues for growth. This book (Book 1 of a collection of three books) is designed to guide readers through the essential principles, practices and methodologies required to navigate the complex world of digital solution development.

The journey begins with an exploration of what digital solutions are, their key characteristics and the profound impact they have on businesses and individuals. From there, the book delves into the critical relationship between digital solutions and business systems, emphasising the importance of aligning technology with organisational objectives. Readers will discover the various approaches to acquiring digital solutions, ranging from bespoke development to leveraging off-the-shelf products and cloud-based services.

Central to the book is the recognition that successful digital solution development requires a deep understanding of business needs, robust Requirements Engineering, and the effective use of models and tools. By addressing these areas, the book equips readers with the knowledge to manage backlogs, model complex systems and adopt software tools that enhance collaboration and innovation.

Written in an easy to understand style, supported by an extensive online glossary (bcs.org/books/ddsglossary/) to help the reader get to grips with the esoteric vocabulary of digital solutions, *Defining Digital Solutions* serves as a comprehensive resource for a broad range of readers (see *Who Is This Book For?* below) wishing to delve deeper into the dark art of digital solution development, and engage more effectively in the development and delivery of digital solutions. It bridges the gap between business strategy and technological execution, offering practical guidance and real-world examples to illustrate best practices.

Whether you are a seasoned professional or a newcomer to the field, this book – and its companions in the series, *Designing Digital Solutions* and *Delivering Digital Solutions* – will empower you to participate in the definition, design, development and delivery of digital solutions that meet the demands of a dynamic and ever-changing world. By embracing the concepts and frameworks outlined herein, you will be well-equipped to drive meaningful change and create lasting value through technology.

WHO IS THIS BOOK FOR?

When the idea for the *Digital Solutions Collection* was originally conceived, the following categories of reader were envisaged:

- **Business analysts (BAs)**: BAs play a crucial role in bridging the gap between business needs and technical solutions, and often work with, or as part of, solution development teams. This book provides an insight into how the complementary disciplines of business analysis and solution development work together to address the needs of an enterprise, and offers frameworks for understanding digital solutions, conducting Requirements Engineering and aligning solutions with organisational goals.

- **Project managers and delivery managers**: This book considers the various options for acquiring digital solutions and provides insights into managing the life cycle of digital solutions, from inception to decommissioning, Agile methodologies, risk management and alignment with strategic objectives.

- **Product managers**: This book helps product managers to understand how to define, prioritise and manage digital solutions to deliver maximum business benefit. It also covers methods to align product backlogs with strategic objectives.

- **Delivery managers (DMs)**: DMs oversee the execution of digital projects. This book offers frameworks for delivering incremental solutions that realise business benefits, handling iterative development cycles and ensuring stakeholder satisfaction.

- **IT managers (ITMs)**: ITMs are responsible for aligning technology with business objectives. This book provides strategies for choosing, implementing and maintaining digital solutions effectively.

- **Solution developers, testers and technical stakeholders**: This book provides an understanding of the entire life cycle of a digital solution, emphasising the broader business context in which these solutions are developed. It explores how various roles and disciplines collaborate to conceive, define, design, develop, test and deliver digital solutions that meet organisational needs while offering value to its customers.

- **Business stakeholders**: Increasingly business stakeholders (product owners, business managers, end-users and subject-matter experts) are being asked to be active participants in the development of digital solutions. This is intrinsically the case where developments follow an Agile methodology that relies on their continuous, active involvement throughout the digital solution life cycle. This book helps business stakeholders to understand how their role fits into digital solution development projects, and also provides further context for the use of digital solutions to address business needs and drive innovation.

- **Students on university and other courses studying digital business change**: This book offers a comprehensive guide to the digital solution life cycle, making it essential for students in business analysis, IT, software development and digital transformation. It provides practical frameworks such as Requirements Engineering and backlog management, preparing students for real-world projects, internships and roles such as BA, software developer and project manager. With a focus on contemporary practices including Agile, cloud solutions and collaborative tools, the book equips students with the skills needed to thrive in a rapidly evolving, innovation-driven industry while emphasising the strategic alignment of solutions with organisational goals.

- **Candidates studying for the BCS International Diploma in Solution Development**, looking for a body of knowledge that covers the breadth of the diploma syllabus and also a range of associated certificates within the diploma scheme.

HOW TO USE THIS BOOK

This book can be used in a number of ways:

- It can be read from cover to cover to provide a good general understanding of the subject, especially for those with little previous exposure to digital solutions.

- Each chapter also stands alone to provide a detailed reference guide to specific aspects of digital solutions, so the reader can choose to dip into the chapters in any order. However, it is recommended that Chapter 1 is read first to provide context for the remaining chapters.

- If more detail is desired after digesting the content of this book, readers can pursue specific topics via the references and further reading section.

HOW THIS BOOK IS ORGANISED

The book is structured into nine chapters, as follows:

- **Chapter 1: What Is a Digital Solution?** This chapter introduces the concept of digital solutions, focusing on their role in addressing problems, improving processes and providing new capabilities through technology. It defines key characteristics of digital solutions, such as being technology-driven, scalable and data-centric. Additionally, it explores their benefits, such as enhanced efficiency and customer experience, and outlines their life cycle from inception to decommissioning.

- **Chapter 2: The Business Context for Digital Solutions**: This chapter emphasises the need to align digital solutions with business objectives. It introduces the POPIT model, which examines the interplay of people, processes, organisational factors, information and technology. Key factors influencing digital investments, such as market conditions and customer expectations, are discussed. The chapter also introduces the business change life cycle (BCLC) to align solutions with organisational transformations.

- **Chapter 3: Acquiring Digital Solutions**: This chapter explores various approaches to acquiring digital solutions, including bespoke development, off-the-shelf products, software as a service and open-source options. It discusses the trade-offs between speed, cost and customisation, while emphasising the importance of aligning solutions with strategic objectives. Emerging trends like low-code and no-code platforms are also highlighted.

- **Chapter 4: Bespoke Development**: This chapter delves into bespoke software development, comparing defined approaches (linear and requirements-driven) with empirical approaches (iterative and adaptive). It highlights the value of Agile practices, incremental delivery and stakeholder collaboration in delivering tailored solutions.

- **Chapter 5: Requirements Engineering**: This chapter introduces a framework and set of best practices for defining and managing requirements for digital solutions. Techniques for requirements elicitation, analysis, validation, and management are covered, emphasising their importance in ensuring the solution aligns with business goals. Critical roles such as BA, product owner, subject-matter expert, project manager and project sponsor are also discussed.

- **Chapter 6: Managing Requirements with Backlogs**: This chapter focuses on backlog management in Agile projects. It explains tools such as user story maps and techniques for prioritising and refining backlogs. The importance of maintaining a clear and adaptable backlog to facilitate iterative development is highlighted.

- **Chapter 7: Modelling the Required Solution**: This chapter explores the role of modelling in the specification of digital solutions, considering modelling notations for defining functionality, data and dynamic system behaviour, emphasising the use of techniques to create accurate, cross-referenced models that guide solution development.

- **Chapter 8: Software Tools to Support Digital Solution Definition**: This chapter reviews software tools that support various activities and disciplines associated with digital solution definition, including collaboration, project management, prototyping and systems modelling. It underscores the importance of selecting the right tools to streamline development processes.

- **Chapter 9: Designing and Delivering Digital Solutions**: This chapter summarises what the earlier chapters have covered and provides a short preview of Book 2: *Designing Digital Solutions*.

Peter Thompson
January 2025

1 WHAT IS A DIGITAL SOLUTION?

The term 'digital' has become synonymous with the technological revolution that has transformed communication, information access and many aspects of our lives. However, it has a surprisingly long history: according to the *Oxford English Dictionary*, the earliest evidence of the word dates back to the 15th century, though at that time it referred to a whole number less than 10. This meaning likely stemmed from the use of fingers (digits) to count. Today, the term has two main meanings:

1. **Relating to numbers and electronic systems**: In this sense, 'digital' refers to using numbers, especially the binary digits 0 and 1, to represent information. This is the foundation of modern computing and electronic devices. Digital data is contrasted with analogue data, which represents information using continuous signals. For example, vinyl records use an analogue signal to store sound, while digital music files use a series of 0s and 1s. Other examples in this context are 'digital device' (e.g. digital camera, digital watch) and 'digital download'.

2. **Relating to technology and the internet**: In this broader sense, 'digital' refers to anything related to computers, the internet and electronic technology. It encompasses the various tools, devices and services that rely on digital information processing. Examples in this context are 'digital marketing' and 'digital business design'.

While there are potentially numerous definitions of 'digital solution', in the context of this book a digital solution is defined as:

A way of using computer technology to address a problem, improve a process or provide new capabilities, that leverages software and hardware to make things more efficient, convenient or effective, enhancing user experiences and driving innovation.

Digital solutions can be found everywhere from smartphones to customer service chatbots, to inventory management systems and self-driving cars. They can streamline tasks, improve communication, enhance data analysis – the list goes on.

While digital solutions are not just about software, this book focuses predominantly on software solutions.

KEY CHARACTERISTICS OF A DIGITAL SOLUTION

Although the definition provided above is incredibly broad and encapsulates a vast range of different solutions – including software applications, cloud computing, artificial intelligence, data analytics and the Internet of Things (IoT) – there are certain characteristics that are common to almost all digital solutions:

- **Technology-driven**: They rely on digital technologies to target specific challenges, inefficiencies or business opportunities.
- **Problem-solving**: They are designed to solve a particular problem, improve efficiency, enhance user experience or enable new capabilities.
- **Automation and efficiency**: They automate manual processes, reduce time taken to undertake tasks and reduce consumption of non-digital resources.
- **Data-centric**: Many digital solutions are powered by data, utilising analytics, machine learning or artificial intelligence (AI) to provide insights, predictions and optimisation.
- **Scalability**: Digital solutions can often scale easily to accommodate growing user bases, increased data or higher demand.

BENEFITS OF DIGITAL SOLUTIONS

Digital solutions can provide organisations and individuals with a range of benefits, including:

- **Communication**: They can provide more accurate and timelier (in most cases) information to individuals, organisations and their customers.
- **Efficiency**: They can automate tasks, reduce manual work and save time.
- **Accuracy**: Automation can reduce human errors and improve data quality.
- **Improved decision-making**: Digital solutions often provide real-time data analytics and insights, helping organisations and users to make better informed decisions.
- **Enhanced customer experience**: Many digital solutions focus on improving user interfaces, personalisation and access to services, providing better customer service, support or interaction, and enhancing the overall customer experience.
- **Cost savings**: By automating tasks and improving efficiency, digital solutions can reduce operational costs.
- **Scalability and flexibility**: Digital solutions are typically easier to scale, allowing businesses to adapt to changing demands quickly.
- **Global reach**: Cloud-based and internet-driven solutions can be accessed globally, enabling businesses to serve customers and users worldwide.

Overall, digital solutions are a powerful way to leverage technology to address modern-day needs and create a more efficient and effective world.

TYPES OF DIGITAL SOLUTION

Digital solutions come in various forms, tailored to solve specific problems, enhance customer experiences and drive innovation. Organisations can leverage these solutions to stay competitive, improve efficiency and deliver valuable products and services to their customers.

Some of the more popular types of digital solution are explored below. These are not mutually exclusive.

Web applications

Web applications are software solutions that run on web browsers. They are accessible via the internet and do not require installation on users' devices. Their uses range from online shopping and content publishing to customer support and data analytics.

Examples of web applications are:

- **ecommerce platforms** (e.g. Shopify and Amazon), which facilitate online sales and transactions;
- **customer relationship management (CRM) systems** (e.g. Salesforce and Microsoft Dynamics 365), which facilitate the management of customer data and interactions; and
- **content management systems (CMS)** (e.g. WordPress and Drupal), which enable users to create, manage and publish digital content.

Mobile applications

Mobile applications (apps) are designed for smartphones and tablet computers. They can be native apps (built for specific operating systems such as iOS or Android), web apps or hybrid apps (a mix of native and web technologies). Their uses range from social networking and mobile banking to online learning and fitness tracking.

Examples of mobile applications are:

- **social media apps** (e.g. WhatsApp and Instagram), which connect users for content sharing and communication;
- **banking apps** (all mainstream banks have these), which enable mobile banking and financial transactions; and
- **productivity and collaboration apps** (e.g. Evernote and Microsoft Teams), which help users to manage tasks and collaborate. These apps are often available through a range of platforms, not just as mobile apps.

Cloud solutions

Cloud solutions provide on-demand access to computing resources (such as storage, servers and applications) over the internet. They offer scalability, flexibility and cost savings. Their uses are diverse and range from the kinds of applications mentioned above, to software development and data storage, to business analytics and machine learning.

Examples of cloud solutions are:

- **Software as a service (SaaS)** (e.g. Microsoft 365, Google Workspace and Salesforce), which provides software applications hosted in the cloud;
- **Platform as a service (PaaS)** (e.g. Microsoft Azure App Service, AWS (Amazon Web Services) Elastic Beanstalk, Heroku, Oracle Cloud Platform and Google App Engine), which provides a platform for developers to build, test, deploy and manage applications in the cloud; and
- **Infrastructure as a service (IaaS)** (e.g. Google Cloud Platform, IBM Cloud, Microsoft Azure and DigitalOcean), which provides virtualised computing resources such as servers and storage, enabling organisations to create their own custom infrastructure.

Enterprise resource planning systems

Enterprise resource planning (ERP) systems integrate multiple business processes into a single unified system. They provide a central database for managing operations such as finance, human resources, procurement, supply chain and manufacturing.

Examples of ERP systems are:

- **SAP ERP**, a comprehensive ERP solution for large enterprises;
- **Oracle NetSuite**, a cloud-based ERP for small and medium-sized businesses; and
- **Microsoft Dynamics 365**, which offers ERP and CRM capabilities.

Artificial intelligence solutions

Artificial intelligence (AI) solutions use a range of state-of-the-art computing technologies (e.g. object recognition, machine learning, natural language processing, speech recognition and synthesis and data analytics) to automate tasks, control smart devices, make predictions and enhance decision-making, among many other functions.

Examples of AI solutions are:

- **Chatbots** (e.g. Zendesk Chat customer service chatbot and Sephora's chatbot – a virtual shopping assistant), which automate customer interactions and provide instant responses to user queries. Chatbots can handle common questions, support services and guide users through processes.
- **Generative AI** (e.g. ChatGPT for writing assistance, DALL-E for creating digital art and GitHub Copilot for programming assistance), which create new content such as text, images, music and videos using AI models. Generative AI is used for creative tasks, content generation and enhancing productivity.

- **Recommendation engines** (e.g. Netflix's personalised movie recommendations and Amazon's 'Customers who bought this also bought ...'), which provide personalised content and product recommendations based on user preferences and behaviour. They are widely used in ecommerce, streaming services and social media.

- **Predictive analytics** (e.g. Salesforce Einstein Analytics for sales forecasting, SAP Predictive Analytics for customer churn prediction and FICO's credit scoring for financial risk assessment), which analyse historical data to make predictions about future events or trends, helping businesses to make informed decisions and anticipate changes.

- **Robotics** (e.g. ABB's robotic arms for assembly lines (industrial robots) and the da Vinci Surgical System for robotic-assisted surgery (medical robots)), which automate physical tasks using AI-driven robots, and can range from industrial robots in manufacturing to robots in healthcare and service industries.

- **Autonomous vehicles** (e.g. Tesla's Autopilot, Waymo's autonomous taxis and Amazon Prime Air delivery drones), which enable self-driving cars and drones to navigate and operate without human intervention, using AI for perception, decision-making and control.

- **Intelligent personal assistants** (e.g. Amazon Alexa, Apple Siri and Google Assistant), which enhance productivity and user convenience by assisting users with tasks, providing information and managing schedules through voice commands or text input.

- **Cybersecurity threat detection** (e.g. Darktrace's intrusion detection system and CrowdStrike's Falcon malware detection platform), which helps to protect data and networks from malicious activity by using AI to analyse patterns and identify anomalies to detect cyber threats and prevent cyberattacks.

- **Fraud detection** (e.g. Visa's credit card fraud prevention platform and Signifyd's fraud protection for online retailers), which identify and prevent fraudulent activities in real time using AI algorithms that analyse transactions for unusual patterns.

- **Advanced diagnostics** (e.g. IBM Watson Health for oncology diagnostics and Zebra Medical Vision for X-ray analysis), which uses AI to assist in medical diagnosis, improving accuracy and speed in identifying diseases based on medical data (e.g. imaging and lab results).

- **Digital twins** (e.g. GE's digital twins for turbine performance analysis, Siemens' digital twin technology for building management and Singapore's digital twin for urban planning), which create a virtual replica of a physical asset or system using real-time data, allowing for simulations, monitoring and optimisation.

Internet of Things solutions

Internet of Things (IoT) solutions connect physical devices to the internet, allowing them to collect, exchange and analyse data. They often involve sensors, smart devices and cloud computing. Their uses range from energy efficiency and healthcare monitoring to supply chain management and smart cities.

Examples of IoT solutions are:

- **smart home systems** (e.g. Google Nest and Amazon Alexa), which automate home functions such as lighting and temperature control;
- **industrial IoT**, which monitors equipment and processes in manufacturing for predictive maintenance; and
- **wearable devices** (e.g. Fitbit and Apple Watch), which track health and fitness metrics.

Data analytics and business intelligence solutions

Data analytics and business intelligence (BI) solutions gather, process and analyse large volumes of data to provide actionable insights for decision-making. Their uses range from sales performance analysis and financial forecasting to driving operational efficiencies and strategic decision- and policy-making (such as during the COVID-19 pandemic).

Examples of data analytics and BI solutions solutions are:

- **BI tools** (e.g. Power BI and Tableau), which visualise data and create reports for operational and strategic decision-making;
- **'big data' solutions** (e.g. Apache Hadoop and Apache Spark), which handle massive datasets for in-depth analytics; and
- **data warehousing** (e.g. Snowflake and Amazon Redshift), which stores and organises data from multiple sources.

Cybersecurity solutions

Cybersecurity solutions protect digital assets from cyber threats, including data breaches, malware and unauthorised access. Their uses range from data protection and threat detection to user authentication and regulatory compliance.

Examples of cybersecurity solutions are:

- **firewalls and antivirus software** (e.g. Windows Defender, Norton Antivirus Plus and McAfee Total Protection), which protect computer systems from malware, viruses and unauthorised access;
- **identity and access management (IAM)** (e.g. Microsoft Azure Active Directory, Google Cloud Identify, IBM Security Verify and AWS Identity and Access Management), which control user access and authentication; and
- **encryption tools** (e.g. BitLocker, VeraCrypt and OpenSSL), which help to protect sensitive data by encoding it so that only authorised parties can access it.

Digital marketing solutions

Digital marketing solutions help businesses to promote their products and services online, leveraging tools and platforms for targeted marketing and analytics. Their uses range from lead generation and brand awareness to customer engagement and market analysis.

Examples of digital marketing solutions are:

- **search engine optimisation (SEO) tools** (e.g. SEMrush, Google Analytics and Moz Pro), which help website owners, digital marketers and content creators to improve their online visibility, analyse website performance, optimise content and track keyword rankings;
- **email marketing platforms** (e.g. Mailchimp and Constant Contact), which help businesses and marketers to manage email campaigns, automate messaging, segment audiences and analyse performance; and
- **social media management tools** (e.g. Hootsuite and Buffer), which help businesses and marketers to streamline their social media activities, including content scheduling, monitoring, analytics and engagement.

Process automation solutions

Automation solutions streamline repetitive tasks and processes using software robots or scripts, freeing up human resources for more strategic work. Their uses range from invoice processing and customer onboarding to data migration and IT service desk automation.

Examples of automation solutions are:

- **workflow automation** (e.g. Zapier, Microsoft Power Automate and Monday.com), which help to streamline business processes by automating repetitive tasks, reducing manual effort, and improving efficiency, without the need to write program code; and
- **RPA tools** (e.g. UiPath, Blue Prism and Pega RPA), which automate repetitive, rule-based tasks in various business processes.

A digital solution is likely to include solution components that are full systems in their own right (as described above) and to connect to other systems as part of its function.

THE LIFE CYCLE OF A DIGITAL SOLUTION

The life cycle of a digital solution (also known as the application life cycle) is iterative and dynamic, requiring continuous adaptation to changes in technology, user needs and business objectives. It encompasses the stages from initial concept and development through deployment and ongoing management, and concludes with retirement or replacement. These stages are illustrated in Figure 1.1 and detailed below.

Inception

The inception stage (also known as discovery) is where the business need or opportunity is identified, and the goals for a digital solution are established. This stage often involves conducting market research and feasibility studies, resulting in the development of

7

Figure 1.1 Life cycle of a digital solution (application life cycle)

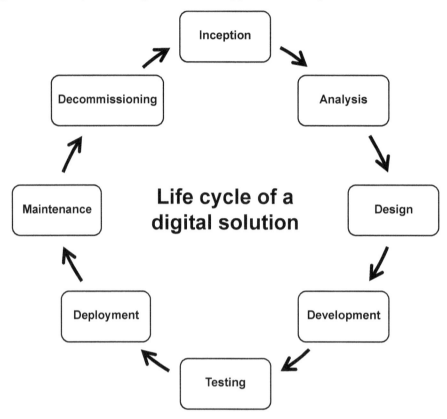

a business case. If the business case is approved by the relevant business sponsor, inception will also incorporate project initiation.

Project initiation involves the definition of high-level business and project objectives, scope and constraints that restrict the project in some way (e.g. timelines, budget, technology, standards and legislation). This results in the development of a Project Initiation Document (PID) or terms of reference (ToR) document, which would also identify the project authority (project sponsor) for decision-making, as well as available resources. It is also common to produce a high-level plan for the development of the digital solution and perform a project risk assessment during project initiation.

Analysis

During the analysis stage, detailed solution requirements are elaborated from the high-level business requirements identified during inception. This stage is often the first stage of a digital solution development project, and is described in more detail in Part II of this book.

Design

The design stage translates the solution requirements defined during the analysis stage into a set of design blueprints that specify how the requirements shall be realised during solution development. These blueprints are used by solution developers to build runtime platforms and executable software that comprise the working digital solution. Design is the subject of Book 2 of this series, *Designing Digital Solutions*.

Development

The development stage is where software developers translate the design blueprints into working software. Development involves a series of sub-stages where the developer (or software engineer) writes program code using one or more programming languages, and compiles it into a computer readable and executable form. This also involves a process known as linking, to link together a set of executable program modules into the final software system.

Testing

During the testing stage the working solution created in the development stage is subjected to a range of different tests to ensure that it works correctly (according to the specifications produced during the design stage), conforms to the functional and non-functional solution requirements (see Chapter 5) defined during the analysis stage, satisfies the business needs (identified in the inception stage) and meets predefined quality criteria. Upon successful completion of the testing stage, the digital solution is ready for deployment and live operational use.

Deployment

The deployment stage is where the digital solution is transferred from the development environment into a production environment, which makes it available to users for live operational use. With the advent of Agile development and increasing pressures to deliver digital solutions quickly and continuously, DevOps practices that automate the transition from development to live operation have become commonplace.

Maintenance

Maintenance involves making changes to the digital solution after it becomes operational. This stage encompasses the continuous use and optimisation of the solution throughout its life until it is decommissioned. Activities during maintenance include addressing defects identified during live use, modifying the solution's functionality to meet evolving requirements, implementing new features and enhancing usability and performance based on insights from ongoing monitoring. The goal is to ensure the solution remains effective and continues to meet the needs of users and the organisation.

Decommissioning

Decommissioning is the final stage in the life cycle of a digital solution, during which the solution is retired from operational use. This occurs when the solution becomes outdated, no longer satisfies the business needs or is replaced by a more suitable alternative. This stage focuses on ensuring a seamless transition away from the existing solution or to its replacement, while taking all necessary precautions to minimise risks and safeguard critical data.

There is often a distinction between the original development project and what is commonly known as 'business as usual'. The latter relates to the life cycle stages after deployment. These two aspects may involve different teams. However, where the solution is developed using an Agile methodology (see Chapter 4) it is quite common for a development team to be assigned to the *product* (for the duration of its life cycle), rather than just the initial development *project*, and the same team works on the development and maintenance of the product throughout its life, as an ongoing series of iterative development cycles and incremental deliveries.

PART I THE CONTEXT FOR DIGITAL SOLUTIONS

2   THE BUSINESS CONTEXT FOR DIGITAL SOLUTIONS

INTRODUCTION

Digital solutions are often developed with a primarily technological focus, which can lose sight of the original business drivers that led to the need for a digital solution in the first place. Understanding the business drivers for the change provides a crucial context for a digital solution development project, which ensures the business needs are fully addressed by the solution.

THE RELATIONSHIP BETWEEN DIGITAL SOLUTIONS AND BUSINESS SYSTEMS

Before exploring the relationship between digital solutions and business systems, it is necessary to understand what a business system is.

As the name implies, a business system is a particular kind of system. The *Oxford English Dictionary* defines a system as:

> A set of things working together as parts of a mechanism or an interconnecting network; a complex whole.

Systems have three key characteristics:

- **an underlying rationale**, which is an underpinning set of values and beliefs that explain why it exists and what it is designed to do;
- **interacting elements** comprising several components that work together to deliver its product, service or outcome; and
- **emergent properties**, which are the properties or outcomes that result from the system as a whole.

In the context of a **business system**, the underlying rationale is often defined in the organisation's mission statement. For example, according to aboutamazon.com, the mission statement for Amazon (as of November 2024) is:

> To be Earth's most customer-centric company, Earth's best employer, and Earth's safest place to work.

A useful framework for understanding the interacting elements of a business system is the POPIT model, developed by Assist Knowledge Development, which is shown in Figure 2.1.

Figure 2.1 The POPIT model (© Assist Knowledge Development Ltd)

The POPIT model identifies five key elements that interact in a business system to produce the emergent properties of the system:

People   The knowledge and skills required of those working within the organisation.

Organisation   The structure, culture and business model of the organisation, and the roles defined to carry out the work of the organisation.

Processes   The business processes applied to carry out the work of the organisation.

Information   The data and information captured, recorded and used by the organisation.

Technology   The technology used to support and conduct the work of the organisation.

Digital solutions are implemented within business systems to support the information and technology needs – although not all technologies within a business system are digital technologies. They do this in various ways, including:

- **Automation of processes**: Digital solutions (e.g. robotic process automation (RPA) and workflow automation tools) can streamline repetitive tasks, reducing manual effort and minimising errors. Additionally, ERP and CRM systems can integrate with automation tools to enhance efficiency in processes such as stock management, logistics, order fulfilment and customer onboarding.

- **Data integration and analytics**: Digital solutions enable more effective data integration, enabling business systems to connect and exchange data seamlessly across different departments (such as integrating CRM with ERP systems). Data analytics platforms and BI tools provide insights that help business systems to make informed decisions. For example, integrating a BI tool with an ERP system can help to analyse financial data and optimise resource allocation.

- **Enhanced customer experience**: Digital solutions such as ecommerce platforms, chatbots and mobile apps can be used to improve the customer experience by providing a more responsive, personalised service. When integrated with CRM systems, these solutions offer a comprehensive view of customer interactions, enabling businesses to tailor their services and respond effectively to customer needs.

- **Scalability and flexibility**: Cloud-based digital solutions (e.g. SaaS platforms such as Salesforce or Microsoft 365) offer scalability, allowing business systems to grow with the organisation's needs without significant infrastructure changes. Business systems can leverage cloud solutions to enhance collaboration, remote work capabilities and global access to data.

- **Improved decision-making**: Digital solutions powered by AI and machine learning help business systems to analyse vast amounts of data in real time, identifying trends and predicting future outcomes. For instance, integrating predictive analytics with ERP or CRM systems can help to anticipate customer demand, optimise inventory levels and reduce costs.

FACTORS INFLUENCING INVESTMENT IN DIGITAL SOLUTION DEVELOPMENT

Investment in digital solutions is a strategic decision influenced by a combination of factors. Some of the more commonplace factors are:

- **Business objectives and strategy**: Organisations are more likely to invest in digital solutions that directly support their strategic objectives, such as improving efficiency, enhancing customer experience or enabling scalability. Additionally, businesses often invest in digital solutions to differentiate themselves in the market, offering unique value propositions.

- **Financial considerations**: The organisation's financial health and allocated budget play a significant role in determining investment capacity. Expected return on investment (ROI), including cost savings, revenue generation or improved productivity, heavily influence investment decisions. Consideration of the total cost of ownership (TCO), including implementation, maintenance, licensing and training costs, must also be considered.

- **Technology trends**: Emerging technologies such as AI, IoT, blockchain and cloud computing drive investments in innovative solutions. The desire to keep up with technological developments to remain competitive and compliant with industry norms is often a key driver.

- **Customer expectations**: Rising customer expectations for convenience, speed and personalisation drive investments in digital tools such as ecommerce platforms, mobile apps and CRM systems. Customer feedback influences investments in solutions that enhance engagement and satisfaction.

- **Regulatory and compliance requirements**: Data protection legislation (e.g. the European General Data Protection Regulation (GDPR)) and industry-specific regulations often necessitate investments in secure and compliant digital solutions.

- **Economic and market conditions**: During economic downturns, organisations may limit spending, while economic growth often encourages investment. Industries experiencing rapid change or high disruption (e.g. retail, healthcare and finance) often invest heavily in digital solutions to adapt and compete.

- **Competitor actions**: Competitor adoption of advanced technologies or digital tools can drive organisations to invest in similar or superior solutions.

- **Organisational readiness**: An organisation's existing infrastructure, workforce skills, culture and ability to handle organisational change (including training employees and adapting processes and workflows) are key influences in investment decisions.

- **Time to market**: The ability to adapt and scale solutions as the business environment changes (see below) is a key influencing factor. Solutions that can be implemented quickly to address immediate needs or seize opportunities are more likely to be pursued.

- **Environmental, social and governance (ESG) considerations**: Investments may be influenced by a desire to adopt solutions that reduce environmental impact (e.g. energy-efficient data centres) to further the organisation's sustainability goals. Digital solutions that align with ethical practices, accessibility and inclusivity are gaining importance, as organisations adopt social responsibility goals.

- **Risk management**: Concerns about data breaches and cyber threats influence investments in secure and resilient digital solutions. Solutions that mitigate risks related to cybersecurity, fraud and regulatory penalties tend to be given priority.

Business environment factors

Decisions regarding investment in digital solutions, and any significant business change for that matter, are often aided by the use of business environment analysis techniques. Commonly used by BAs, these techniques help organisations to identify strengths, weaknesses, opportunities and threats. Strengths and weaknesses are identified by using *internal* environment analysis techniques, while opportunities and threats are identified using *external* environment analysis techniques.

A technique that is widely used to analyse the external environment is PESTLE, illustrated in Figure 2.2 and discussed below.

Figure 2.2 PESTLE factors

Political	The political situation in the country in which an organisation operates can have positive or negative impacts. For example, there may be a change of government and new policies may be introduced. The international situation is relevant, too, and may affect such things as energy costs, the availability of materials and the ability to trade in certain areas.
Economic	The state of the economy, both nationally and internationally. The economy may be booming or in a recession, and the organisation must respond to that. Public sector and charitable organisations may be affected as well as private sector organisations. For example, a downturn in the economy may result in lower tax revenue or reduced charitable contributions.
Socio-cultural	Societal demographics, trends and changing social attitudes. An ageing population, for example, will place more demands on public services, whereas a young population may make the adoption of products based on new technologies easier.
Technological	New technologies come along all the time, and older ones become obsolete, and organisations must respond to that. An obvious current example is AI, where governments and organisations are working out how to adopt the new technology to provide new products and services, and how the new technology can be leveraged for greater operational efficiency and effectiveness.
Legal	Legislation reflects politicians' wishes, but this category also includes entities such as regulators who may adopt a 'light touch' or a more intrusive approach, depending on the circumstances. Changes in legislation and regulations are common drivers for investment in digital solutions.

Environmental   This category focuses on the natural environment within which we live, and organisations' desires to address 'green' issues, which may, at least in part, be influenced by socio-cultural factors. One area that is prominent in people's minds these days is the widespread concerns over climate change. Organisations must therefore consider how best they can contribute to combating climate change, reducing waste and their 'carbon footprint'.

Organisations cannot usually do much to change these external factors, although they might take action such as lobbying governments to change the political climate. The key thing is that organisations must identify changes in the external environment – be they threats or opportunities – and work out how best to adapt to them.

In addition to these external factors, organisations must look internally to see where digital solutions might enable them to become more effective or efficient. One way of thinking about this is to consider what resources the organisation has available to it and how effective they are. This resource audit is illustrated in Figure 2.3.

Figure 2.3 Resource audit

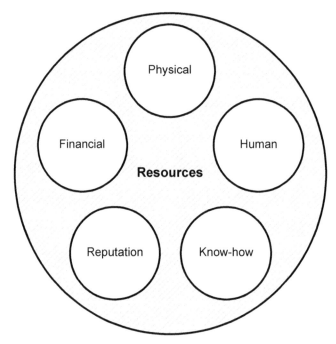

The resources considered are:

Physical   This includes land, buildings, vehicles, machinery, computers and office fixtures and fittings. These may range from modern, efficient and state-of-the-art to old, obsolete and requiring significant – and often costly – maintenance.

Financial   A commercial organisation may have strong capital reserves that could be invested in change projects and, in particular, new digital solutions, or it may have no spare capital for investment. It may have a good credit rating, and so be able to borrow money when needed, or a poor one. A public sector organisation will depend on tax revenues and what share of those it can obtain.

Human   The workforce may be highly skilled and motivated or it may be demoralised. Staff may be hard to find and expensive to hire and retain.

Know-how   This is the collective knowledge of the organisation, manifested in well-developed methods and processes and sometimes reflected in patents and other intellectual property. Know-how can be embodied in organisational artefacts and protected for the future or lost when key employees leave the organisation.

Reputation   The organisation may have a good reputation with the public (or a strong brand), or it may not. A good reputation must be defended and a poor one is hard to shake off.

The resource audit factors enable an organisation to identify and understand its strengths and weaknesses.

Organisations typically prioritise change initiatives that pursue business opportunities or avoid or mitigate threats, or help to overcome their weaknesses. They may also favour initiatives that play to their strengths.

DIGITAL SOLUTION DEVELOPMENT WITHIN THE BUSINESS CHANGE LIFE CYCLE

The business change life cycle (BCLC) is a framework that comprises the stages an organisation undertakes to plan, implement and sustain change to achieve strategic objectives. It aligns the development of digital solutions with the broader scope of organisational transformation, ensuring that technology investments deliver measurable business benefits.

Digital solution development represents the technological backbone of the BCLC and plays a critical role in enabling successful organisational transformation. By aligning digital solutions with each stage of the life cycle, organisations can ensure their investments promote meaningful and sustainable business change.

Figure 2.4 presents a diagrammatic representation of the BCLC, and the various stages are described below.

Figure 2.4 The business change life cycle (© Assist Knowledge Development Ltd)

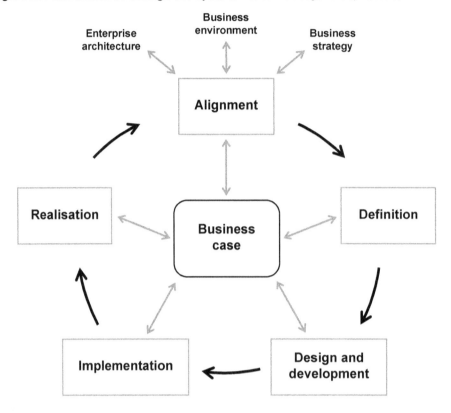

Alignment   The alignment stage of the BCLC is concerned with ensuring that any proposed change initiatives align with three areas relevant to the organisation: the external environment, the business strategy and the enterprise architecture. Techniques such as PESTLE may be used to analyse the factors in the external environment within which the organisation operates. The work conducted during the alignment stage also helps to ensure that any external forces or internal strategic decisions are considered and acted upon where relevant.

Definition   This stage is concerned with conducting an analysis of an existing business situation to determine the root causes of any problems, identify any opportunities for development or growth, clarify the high-level business requirements and recommend the changes needed to resolve the problems and grasp the opportunities. A business case that evaluates and justifies the recommended way forward, and determines the programmes and projects required to progress the changes, is developed during this stage. The detailed requirements are defined, should approval be given to progress the recommendations in the business case.

Design and development	This stage involves the detailed design of solutions, some digital and some not (e.g. redesign of the organisation structure and job roles) that are needed to execute the change programmes. Where relevant, this also incorporates the development and testing stages of the life cycle of a digital solution – see Figure 1.1.
Implementation	This is the stage when the business transitions from its old ways of working to the new, which involves putting the developed digital solution(s) into live operation. This corresponds to the *deployment* stage in Figure 1.1.
Realisation	The final stage concerns a review of the benefits that were anticipated (and documented in the business case) as a result of implementing the business changes, to determine whether or not they have been realised. Where the benefits have not been fully realised, this may lead to additional changes to fully realise them. This is represented by the arrow from realisation to alignment.

Figure 2.4 identifies the **business case** at the heart of the BCLC. The business case provides the justification for the proposed changes and also a means of measuring the success of these changes during the realisation stage. The double-headed arrows to and from the business case to each stage reflect the fact that the business case should be reviewed at each stage to ensure that the change programme/project remains aligned to the original rationale, but also that the business case may need to be updated if new information comes to light. The business case in the context of a typical digital solution development project is discussed later in this chapter.

BUSINESS ANALYSIS AND DIGITAL SOLUTION DEVELOPMENT

As Figure 2.4 shows, the BCLC is a continuing process whereby an organisation attempts to stay relevant in a changing environment. The first two stages of the life cycle – alignment and definition – are the province of business analysts (BAs), although BAs have a role to play throughout the life cycle.

Research into business analysis by Dr Debra Paul (2018) has identified that there is a suite of services offered by BAs, which Dr Paul has synthesised into the Business Analysis Service Framework (BASF), shown in Figure 2.5.

Situation investigation and problem analysis involves investigating the concerns, challenges and opportunities that exist within a given business system (or situation), identifying the root causes of problems and where changes may be required and desirable.

Where an organisation is not operating optimally, or is keen to pursue an opportunity presented by the business environment, **feasibility assessment and business case development** involves making recommendations to senior management about what needs to be done to improve efficiency and effectiveness, and developing a business case to explain and justify the recommended changes. The required changes will involve

Figure 2.5 The BASF (Source: Paul, 2018. © Debra Paul)

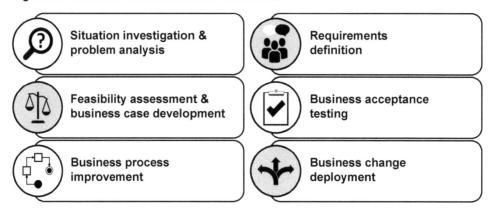

one or more aspects of the organisation represented in the POPIT model shown in Figure 2.1. One area that is often the focus of changes is business processes.

Business process improvement involves BAs researching, analysing, documenting and redesigning business processes. In addition, they apply 'gap analysis' to identify changes to those processes to bring about improvements within the organisation, and identify the actions needed to implement those changes and produce the business benefits.

Requirements definition involves eliciting, analysing and defining the requirements for changes to business processes and for new or enhanced digital solutions. In the case of digital solutions, these requirements form the basis for the design and development, or procurement, of the digital solution. The approach taken by BAs varies according to the development philosophy employed. Where a traditional, linear, approach is being followed, the requirements must be defined in sufficient detail to enable a comprehensive solution design to be produced before software development commences. Where an Agile approach is adopted, the requirements can remain at a relatively high level of detail until they are prioritised for development during a particular development iteration (Sprint), where the detail is added just in time for development to commence. This is discussed in more detail in Chapter 5.

During the development or procurement of a digital solution, **business acceptance testing** involves testing the solution to check that it satisfies the business requirements. During business acceptance testing, BAs can help to define the tests and assist the business stakeholders in running these tests, feeding back the results to the development team. Additionally, BAs assist developers or suppliers as they create the solution, by providing further business context and acting as a liaison between the technical and business stakeholders.

In the final element of the BASF, **business change deployment**, BAs assist in the successful delivery and adoption of the business change solution. They also provide support to the organisation in making sure that the expected business benefits are realised. Supporting the business during the implementation of change can involve providing training in the use of new business processes and digital solutions, and also offering support for the emotional issues encountered during business change, with BAs assisting business stakeholders as they adjust to their new working environment.

MAKING THE BUSINESS CASE FOR DIGITAL SOLUTION DEVELOPMENT

The factors influencing investment in digital solutions were considered earlier in this chapter. However, before pressing ahead with a digital solution development project or the procurement of an off-the-shelf solution, it is essential to first develop a business case, to ensure that resources (including money, time and effort) are invested in solutions that align with the organisation's goals, deliver tangible benefits and address real business needs.

The business case provides a structured justification for acquiring a digital solution to guide the decision to invest, evaluating a range of possible options (see Chapter 3) to ensure that the best option is pursued. For each option considered, the business case should determine the feasibility of progressing that option, along with the expected benefits (including ROI), and an assessment of the risks and impacts associated with implementing the option, so that an informed decision can be made.

The business case in the digital solution development life cycle

Figure 2.6 shows an overview life cycle for a digital solution development project, with a number of 'gateways' at which the business case should be reviewed. A range of alternative life cycle models is explored in Chapter 4.

Figure 2.6 The business case in the life cycle of a digital solution development project (© Assist Knowledge Development Ltd)

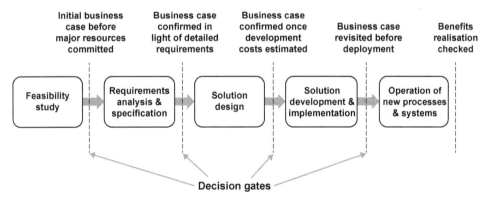

An initial business case is typically prepared after a feasibility study of the proposed project. This corresponds to the **inception** stage in the life cycle of a digital solution (see Figure 1.1). The feasibility study establishes the anticipated outline costs for the project and the expected benefits to be realised from completing it, and determines whether, in principle, the project is worthwhile. If the project is deemed worthwhile at this stage, it is approved and the project team is allowed to move on to more detailed analysis and specification of the requirements. This second stage in Figure 2.6 corresponds to the **analysis** stage in Figure 1.1 and is where Requirements Engineering is conducted (see Chapter 5).

Once the requirements have been elicited and specified, the business case is revisited to check that the costs of the project are still justified by the expected benefits. By this point the solution development team is likely to be able to provide a more accurate assessment of the likely costs of development, based on a clearer understanding of the solution requirements.

With the requirements defined, the project team now has a choice of approaches available to it for acquiring a solution that realises the requirements, as explored in Chapter 3. If a bespoke solution is to be developed, user experience (UX) professionals and solution designers work out how the requirements are to be realised using the hardware and software available, through solution design. Following this, there should be an even more accurate idea of the costs of completing the development work, and therefore there is a need to revisit the business case. If a ready-made solution is to be procured, then vendors would be asked to provide either indicative estimates or definitive quotations for the costs involved. This third stage in Figure 2.6 corresponds to the **design** stage in Figure 1.1.

In the next stage, either the solution is built or it is purchased and, as necessary, customised to meet users' requirements. This stage also includes a variety of tests that are conducted to determine if the solution has been built correctly and is fit for purpose. This fourth stage in Figure 2.6 corresponds to the **development** and **testing** stages in Figure 1.1.

The final stage is to put the solution into live operation, but a further gateway has been shown here because – and especially if the development has taken a long time – it is necessary to check that the business circumstances have not changed, and to assure the organisation that the solution is still needed and fit for purpose. This final stage in Figure 2.6 corresponds to the **deployment** stage in Figure 1.1.

The final use of the business case occurs after the project has been completed. The project sponsor should initiate a benefits review to consider whether the projected benefits have been realised. There are two reasons for this:

1. If some of the benefits have not been achieved, they may still be retrievable and the review should identify what further actions are needed to achieve them.

2. Over time, the organisation gets better at deciding which benefits are achievable or not, and so gets better at selecting which projects have the greatest chance of success. A benefits review can act as a retrospective to learn lessons and improve the organisation's investment appraisal and benefits management capability.

The cone of uncertainty

The above description has considered the need to revise the business case as new information comes to light, especially as the estimate of development costs becomes more accurate due to improved clarity of the scope of the work as development progresses. This concept is known as the cone of uncertainty, and is visualised in Figure 2.7.

Figure 2.7 The cone of uncertainty

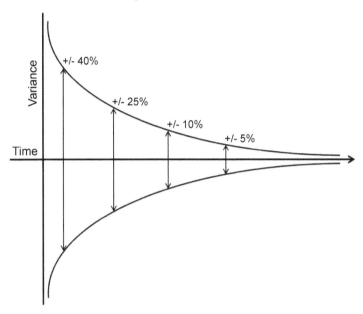

The horizontal axis represents time and the vertical axis the degree of uncertainty, resulting in a potential variance in estimates of ±40 per cent in the early stages of a project. As time progresses, the degree of uncertainty decreases due to more information becoming available.

This is not the only reason to revisit the business case. If there is a significant change in the business environment – for example, a company is the subject of a takeover or there is a change of government – the business case should be checked to ensure the project is still viable in the changed circumstances.

Business case contents

Business cases vary considerably from organisation to organisation, but the following contents are typical:

Introduction	Sets the scene and explains the purpose and structure of the business case.
Management summary	Summarises the nature of the problem or opportunity and options considered, and makes a persuasive case for the recommended course of action. As this is aimed at providing a synopsis of the document for senior managers, it is typically limited to a single side of A4 to enable them to quickly determine whether it is worth investing the time to read the entire document.

Background	Sets out the business background to the proposed initiative and describes the problem that is to be solved, or the opportunity to be pursued.
Options	Provides a list of the options considered with a brief explanation of why some of the options have been discarded and why others have been shortlisted. The shortlisted options (including the 'do nothing' option) are evaluated in more detail, including costs, benefits, a cost–benefit analysis, impact assessment and risk assessment (see below).
Benefits	Identifies the beneficial outcomes the option is expected to achieve, both tangible and intangible.
Costs	Itemises the up-front and ongoing costs of implementing the option.
Impacts	Assesses the anticipated impacts on the organisation as a consequence of implementing the option. The POPIT model is a useful framework for considering impacts holistically (such as impacts on the organisation's people, its processes, its culture and structure).
Risks	Assesses the potential risks associated with implementing the option. For each risk an assessment of its likelihood, severity and impact (if the risk is realised), together with any countermeasures that could be put in place to reduce the likelihood (avoidance actions) or impact (mitigation actions) of the risk.
Investment appraisal	Provides an appraisal of the financial costs and benefits over time, and determines if and when the investment is expected to pay back (breakeven analysis) and the level of profit or loss the option is expected to make (net present value).
Conclusions and recommendations	Concludes the document with a summary of the key insights to be drawn along with a recommendation of which option the author(s) believe should be taken forward. This may be the 'do nothing' option, which effectively suggests that the proposed initiative is not feasible or desirable.
Appendices	To avoid making the body of the business case too unwieldy, detailed information (e.g. technical details of the proposed solution or a detailed breakdown of costs) is often collected in an appendix, where it is available for review if required.

OUTSOURCING AND OFFSHORING DIGITAL SOLUTION DEVELOPMENT

Outsourcing and offshoring are two common strategies organisations use to develop digital solutions by leveraging external resources or international talent. Both approaches offer opportunities to reduce costs, access specialised skills and accelerate development timelines. While the two practices can be deployed individually (one does not necessarily imply the other), they are often combined.

Outsourcing

Outsourcing involves contracting a third-party organisation or service provider to handle the development of a digital solution. The outsourcing partner may be located in the same country as the customer organisation (onshore) or internationally (offshore).

Outsourcing offers some valuable benefits:

- **access to expertise**: enables businesses to tap into the technical expertise and experience (such as cutting-edge technologies) of specialised development teams;
- **cost savings**: reduces overhead expenses, such as salaries, training and infrastructure, compared to maintaining an in-house team;
- **scalability**: enables businesses to quickly scale resources up or down based on project needs; and
- **focus on core activities**: frees up internal teams to focus on strategic initiatives rather than technical development.

However, outsourcing also raises challenges, in particular:

- **communication barriers**: language and knowledge gaps can impede communication;
- **loss of control**: handing over development to a third party may lead to reduced oversight and alignment with business goals as the customer organisation loses direct control of systems that are critical to its business objectives; additionally, knowledge of these key systems resides in the supplier organisation rather than in the customer organisation; and
- **data security risks**: sharing sensitive business information with external teams introduces potential risks, in particular, the risk of data breaches.

An outsourcing contract may cover just the initial development of the digital solution, but sometimes the third-party supplier takes complete responsibility for the organisation's IT systems. Cost is often a driver, but the desire to take control of a spiralling IT budget and to transfer responsibility and risk are also important considerations.

The term **insourcing** is sometimes used to contrast with outsourcing. Insourcing is where tasks, functions or projects are assigned to an organisation's internal team rather than outsourcing them to an external provider. In the context of digital solution development, insourcing involves using in-house resources (such as employees, infrastructure and expertise) to create, manage and maintain digital solutions. The benefits (enhanced control, alignment with organisational goals, knowledge retention, security and confidentiality and faster iterations) and challenges (resource availability, higher initial costs, capacity constraints and limited specialised expertise) are typically the opposite to outsourcing.

Offshoring

Offshoring involves relocating digital solution development activities to teams or service providers in another country, often where labour costs are lower. Many outsourcing providers have offshore teams, but it is also becoming popular for in-house teams within large organisations to be located offshore, to develop solutions in a more cost-effective way.

Common offshoring destinations include:

- **India**, known for its large pool of IT professionals and competitive pricing;
- **Eastern Europe**, where countries such as Ukraine and Poland offer strong technical expertise and proximity to Western markets; and
- **Southeast Asia**, where the Philippines and Vietnam are emerging as cost-effective destinations for software development.

Outsourcing offers some valuable benefits:

- **cost efficiency**: significant savings on labour and operational costs due to differences in wages across countries;
- **global talent pool**: access to a wider range of skilled developers and specialists;
- **24/7 development cycle**: teams in different time zones can enable continuous development, reducing time to market; and
- **currency and tax advantages**: favourable exchange rates or tax benefits may further reduce costs.

Like outsourcing, offshoring has its challenges:

- **cultural differences**: variations in work culture, business practices and communication styles can impact project execution;
- **quality concerns**: inconsistent quality or lack of accountability may arise if the offshore team is not carefully vetted and managed; and
- **legal and regulatory compliance**: ensuring adherence to intellectual property laws, data privacy regulations and labour laws in another country can be complex.

3　ACQUIRING DIGITAL SOLUTIONS

INTRODUCTION

There are a range of approaches to acquiring digital solutions. The approach chosen will reflect:

- the priorities of the organisation;
- the state of its finances;
- the competitive position of the organisation;
- the business and technical skills available;
- the criticality of the solution;
- the urgency of finding a solution; and
- the demands of external entities such as regulators.

OPTIONS FOR ACQUIRING DIGITAL SOLUTIONS

While historically organisations acquired and deployed solutions in isolation, that is rarely the case these days. Instead, the solution is made up of a number of integrated component parts. So, although one of the options presented below could potentially provide the entire solution, it is more likely that the different component parts of an **integrated solution** may be acquired using different options. For example, an organisation may find that there is a commercial off-the-shelf (COTS) package that meets 90 per cent of its needs, and addresses the gap (the unmet needs) with a combination of bespoke and open-source software.

The business case for acquiring a digital solution (see Chapter 2) should consider the factors described in this chapter and balance these against the costs, benefits, impacts and risks offered by the recommended combination.

Bespoke software development

A bespoke solution is created specifically, and probably exclusively, for a particular organisation. Consequently, the solution should meet the organisation's needs exactly (provided they have been defined precisely enough) and should, where relevant, provide it with some competitive advantage. The latter point is especially the case where the organisation has something distinctive about the way it operates that its competitors would find difficult, or impossible, to replicate.

Bespoke solutions offer a number of benefits:

- **Tailored fit**: Bespoke solutions are designed to meet the specific needs and requirements of the organisation, ensuring a perfect fit.
- **Competitive advantage**: Bespoke solutions can incorporate unique features and functionality that differentiates the organisation from its competitors.
- **Integration capability**: Bespoke solutions can be designed to integrate seamlessly with existing systems, especially those built using legacy technologies.
- **Greater efficiency**: Bespoke solutions optimise processes by addressing specific pain points and eliminating unnecessary features.
- **Improved security**: Bespoke solutions can incorporate advanced, tailored security measures to safeguard data.
- **Cost-effectiveness over time**: Although the initial investment may be higher, bespoke solutions can reduce ongoing costs associated with licensing and unused features in off-the-shelf software.
- **Ownership and control**: The customer organisation has full ownership of the solution, enabling flexibility in updates and changes without relying on third-party providers.

There are, however, some notable downsides to bespoke development, including:

- **Cost**: The entire cost of the solution is borne by the organisation commissioning it.
- **Timescale**: It is likely to be time-consuming to develop a bespoke solution and it requires considerable input from management and other staff to do it well.
- **Requirements**: Defining the requirements precisely enough to ensure that the solution meets the business needs is difficult, although the techniques described in Chapter 5 have proved effective in dealing with this problem.

Commercial off-the-shelf solutions

In contrast to the bespoke approach, with the COTS approach the organisation procures a ready-made solution from a vendor and deploys it as-is. The solution is unlikely to be a perfect match to the organisation's needs, and may require some adjustment of working practices, but there are significant advantages:

- **Quicker delivery**: The solution already exists, so a large proportion of the development cycle (design and software engineering) is removed. However, it is still necessary to define clear requirements to ensure that the best available solution to meet the organisation's needs is selected, and acceptance testing is essential.

- **Proven quality**: The solution has been tried, tested and probably improved by previous purchasers.

- **Lower cost of implementation**: The development costs are effectively shared across multiple customer organisations.

- **Lower costs of upgrades**: The cost of providing additional functionality or modifications (e.g. to meet regulatory changes) is shared between all the customer organisations.

- **Readily available support**: Product vendors typically offer a range of support and product maintenance options as part of the package, although the customer organisation needs to negotiate service level agreements to ensure that the level of support and response times meet their needs.

There are also, of course, drawbacks to acquiring a COTS solution, including:

- **Compromise**: No COTS solution is likely to meet the organisation's needs exactly.

- **Changes in working practices**: As a consequence of the previous issue, the organisation may have to change its processes and procedures to match what the package can do.

- **Reliance on the supplier**: The customer organisation is often beholden to the supplier for maintenance and upgrades, so it is essential to ensure that the terms of the provision of such services is agreed prior to procuring the solution. In some situations, this 'lock-in' can be hard to break out of if the product or associated services no longer meet the needs of the organisation.

- **No competitive advantage**: Using a COTS solution will generally not afford the customer organisation any advantage over their competitors, who are free to procure and use the same product.

Modified off-the-shelf solutions

Many organisations when selecting and procuring COTS solutions have found that the compromise issue cited above is just too restrictive to their operation. However, the main alternative (bespoke development) is also prohibitive. This has led to a variation on the COTS approach: modified off-the-shelf (MOTS) solutions. This is similar to the COTS approach but the solution is modified to match the organisation's needs more closely. This clearly makes the solution a better fit for the organisation and reduces the degree to which it must change its operating practices. However, since the modified elements of the solution are different from the standard product, extra costs will be incurred every time there is an update to the standard COTS product to ensure that the customised elements still work properly. If the required modifications are too extensive – it has been suggested that 10–20 per cent might be a maximum – then it will almost certainly be better to consider another option.

Component-based solutions

With a component-based approach, a number of pre-existing pieces of software (software components) are combined to provide the overall solution. Software components can be fine-grained (e.g. a single function to look up an address from a postcode), or more coarse-grained (e.g. an entire application that is combined with other applications to provide a complete solution). Additionally, components can be ready-made (off-the-shelf) or bespoke.

This approach provides a more effective way of addressing the compromise issue encountered with COTS, without the disadvantages of MOTS, by combining a COTS application with bespoke components that address the requirements not met by the off-the-shelf software.

As with off-the-shelf solutions, a big advantage here is speed of delivery, as many, or perhaps all, of the components already exist. In addition, they should have been tested extensively and be more robust than a purely bespoke solution. One difficulty might be that, if the base components are modified in some way, they may not continue to work in the way the organisation wants. Alternatively, the organisation 'freezes' them on installation but, in that case, it will incur all the costs of upgrades as and when they are needed.

A popular approach to software architecture, called microservices, takes the component-based concept to another level. This is explored in *Designing Digital Solutions*.

Building solutions with CRM and ERP platforms

CRM and ERP packages are both based on the concept of **best of breed** because the way they work encapsulates industry best practice. So, by adopting them, the organisation in effect adopts that best practice. This makes sense for certain generic business applications, such as payroll systems, where there is no competitive advantage to be gained from having a bespoke solution. The other advantages of CRM/ERP platforms are similar to those for COTS solutions discussed earlier.

Some CRM/ERP packages are provided as **template solutions**, which can be configured to meet the precise needs of the customer rather than tailoring the actual program code itself, overcoming one of the significant disadvantages of the MOTS approach.

Software as a service

In our modern world many individuals prefer use over ownership in many aspects of their lives: they live in rented property, they lease cars and they hire clothing for special events. Similarly, many suppliers of software have moved from outright purchase to a subscription model, which is the premise behind SaaS.

For an organisation, the advantages are obvious:

- There is no up-front capital cost for the software.
- Regular updates are provided and, as with COTS solutions, the costs are shared between a number of users.

- The organisation avoids having to manage a large solution development workforce.
- Responsibility for the software is delegated to a supplier.
- SaaS solutions are inherently scalable and adding and removing users and additional modules is relatively easy.

The most obvious downside of SaaS, similar to COTS solutions, is that the customer organisation has limited influence over the future development of the software – if the vendor decides to make a major change, the users have little choice, in the short term, but to accept this, and, unlike leasing a car, it is not easy to just send the software back and adopt something else, especially if it has become integral to the organisation's operations.

A further issue concerns the management of the data. It can be more expensive to obtain and migrate the data stored in a SaaS solution when switching suppliers than the original investment in the solution. There is also the complex issue of data ownership and protection with regard to regulatory requirements.

Open-source software

So far, this chapter has considered digital solutions that are proprietary – that is, the copyright in them is owned either by the organisation commissioning the development (for bespoke solutions) or the vendor (for COTS, MOTS, CRM/ERP and SaaS). However, many software applications are now available on an open-source basis, which means that the developers have made their software readily available to anyone who wants to use it. In many cases, open-source software is continuously enhanced and improved by a wide community of developers.

The main benefits of open-source software are therefore:

- the solution is readily available;
- it is provided free of charge;
- it has been widely tested; and
- there is often a community of users from whom support and assistance can be obtained (an alternative approach is to pay for support from an organisation or specialist provider, which can be expensive).

Some organisations will customise open-source software for a fee. For example, an organisation may develop skills in an open-source product (or even be a main contributor). If user organisations need extra features added to the product, the developing organisation will do so in exchange for support fees or a more direct fee-for-features contract.

A common concern when acquiring open-source software components and applications is security, and especially with regard to the data being managed and used by the open-source software. However, in practice, having access to the source code gives organisations more control over security features.

If an organisation wishes to make extensive use of open-source software, they should consider joining and contributing to the developer and user communities (such as fixes for defects, use cases and documentation). This exchange means that the development team knows the experts and can obtain help when needed, and that they are up to date with the latest changes and are able to take advantage of the continuous stream of security fixes needed in modern software due to the persistence of cyberattacks.

No-code/low-code solutions

No-code and low-code development are approaches to software development that aim to simplify and speed up the development process, allowing business change professionals, or even end-users, with limited or no coding skills to build applications. They are designed to make application development accessible to a broader audience, reducing reliance on professional developers and enabling faster development cycles.

No-code and low-code platforms are valuable tools in modern application development, especially for businesses looking to accelerate digital transformation, empower non-technical staff or quickly prototype new ideas. While both approaches help to reduce development time, lower costs and provide business agility, each approach has its own idiosyncrasies, benefits, challenges and use cases, explored below.

No-code development
No-code development platforms enable non-technical stakeholders to create applications without writing any code. They offer a number of features for configuring and building applications:

- A drag-and-drop interface enables users to add and arrange elements by dragging and dropping them onto an application canvas, making it easy to design user interfaces and workflows.

- Pre-built templates and components provide elements such as forms, tables, buttons and layouts that are ready to use.

- Many no-code platforms have built-in integrations with common services (e.g. Google Sheets (a cloud-based spreadsheet application), Slack (a collaborative communication platform that provides channels for organised messaging, file sharing and integrations with other tools) and payment gateways) to simplify data connections and interfaces.

- Automated workflows enable users to set up workflows and business rules without coding, such as sending automated emails or triggering notifications.

No-code development offers a number of benefits:

- **Accessibility**: It enables non-technical users to create applications, lowering the barrier to entry.

- **Speed**: It supports rapid prototyping and development, as users can build applications without the need to write code, which can be very time-consuming.

- **Cost-effective**: It reduces the need for a large development team, which can lower costs for businesses.

Although clearly very beneficial for rapid development of digital solutions, no-code development also has limitations:

- **Limited customisation**: No-code platforms are typically limited to predefined features, making it challenging to create highly customised or complex applications.

- **Scalability issues**: No-code solutions can struggle to scale effectively for high-demand applications.

- **Dependency on a specific platform**: Developers using no-code solutions are often locked into a specific platform, limiting flexibility and control over the application.

Low-code development
Low-code development platforms require minimal coding but still involve some programming to build more complex or customised applications, compared to their no-code equivalents. Like no-code platforms, they offer visual development tools, but also enable users to add custom code to achieve more flexibility. Low-code platforms are often used by professional developers or semi-technical users who want to streamline development but still need more control over functionality and design than no-code platforms provide.

Similar to no-code platforms, low-code platforms use a drag-and-drop interface, but with more flexibility. They also offer pre-built modules or components, but unlike no-code platforms, developers can modify or extend these with custom code. Custom code can also be used to add unique functionality, integrate with external services or for creating complex workflows and business rules that require some coding.

The benefits of low-code development are similar to no-code development, with the following additional benefits:

- **Customisation**: Low-code platforms enable customisation of apps beyond what is possible with no-code platforms, making them more suitable for more complex applications.

- **Complex tasks**: Low-code platforms enable developers to focus on complex tasks while automating repetitive tasks and increasing productivity.

The primary limitation of low-code development is that the platforms are not completely code-free, requiring users to have some programming knowledge for more advanced customisation. Additionally, while low-code development is effective for building simple to moderately complex applications, it may still face challenges when managing very large or highly customised projects.

Table 3.1 provides a summary of the key differences between no-code and low-code development.

Table 3.1 Comparison of no-code and low-code development

Aspect	No-code development	Low-code development
Target audience	Non-technical users (citizen developers)	Semi-technical users and developers
Customisation level	Limited	Moderate to high
Development speed	Very fast	Fast
Coding required	No	Minimal
Scalability	Limited	Moderate
Suitability for complex applications	No	Yes
Dependency on platform	High	Moderate to high
Use cases	• Simple internal tools or dashboards • Marketing or landing pages • Automating workflows between SaaS apps • Simple data entry or reporting applications	• Enterprise applications with custom workflows • Mobile applications with moderate complexity • Business process automation • Prototyping complex applications for rapid iteration

FACTORS INFLUENCING CHOICE OF APPROACH

The choice of approach to acquiring digital solutions depends on several factors, which can vary based on organisational needs, strategic objectives, resources and constraints. Some of the most common considerations are discussed below.

Business needs and objectives	Whether the solution addresses highly specific or general business needs will often determine whether an off-the-shelf solution is available or whether, due to the niche requirements, a bespoke solution is needed.
Time sensitivity/ time to market	The urgency of implementing the solution might favour quicker options such as SaaS, low-code or no-code platforms, which offer faster deployment compared to ERP or bespoke development.
Budget and TCO	The up-front costs for bespoke are high; lower for ERP/CRM or COTS solutions, and lower still for SaaS, open-source, or low-code platforms. SaaS involves ongoing subscription fees, while open-source may have lower operating costs but higher maintenance needs. Proprietary software (e.g. COTS and SaaS) incurs licence fees, while open-source can avoid these but may need more in-house expertise.

Technical requirements	The need to integrate with existing systems may favour COTS, component-based or CRM/ERP solutions. Cloud-based (SaaS) and modular (component-based) solutions can scale more easily than fully bespoke or on-premises (on-prem) systems.
Security and compliance	Organisations with stringent compliance needs might prefer bespoke or open-source solutions to control security features.
Customisation and flexibility	Bespoke and component-based solutions involve a high degree of customisation, followed by MOTS, open-source and low-code, with SaaS, COTS, CRM and ERP solutions requiring the least. The latter are typically highly configurable, tailoring their behaviour to the customer organisation's needs by the setting of a variety of configuration switches rather than customising the program code. Open-source, low-code and component-based solutions are often more adaptable to changing needs.
Resource availability	Open-source and bespoke solutions often require significant in-house technical expertise, whereas SaaS and COTS provide vendor support, reducing dependency on internal resources. Low-code and no-code platforms enable non-technical teams to contribute to digital solution development.
Risk tolerance	SaaS and proprietary COTS solutions (and some ERP and CRM solutions) pose risks of vendor lock-in, where the customer organisation may be so invested in their solutions that it becomes very difficult and expensive to move to another vendor's solution. ERP, CRM and SaaS offerings are generally stable, while bespoke and new open-source tools might involve higher risks. Bespoke and open-source require ongoing maintenance by the organisation or an outsourced development organisation.
Innovation and differentiation	Bespoke and component-based approaches can create unique solutions, while SaaS and ERP/CRM solutions typically provide more generic and industry standard functionality. No-code, low-code and open-source enable quicker innovation cycles for testing ideas.
Vendor and market considerations	SaaS and ERP/CRM vendors with a proven track record provide stability. Open-source solutions often rely on an active developer community. Licensing flexibility, exit options and support agreements can influence the decision regarding the most appropriate option.
Organisational culture	Organisations with a culture of agility may prefer SaaS or low-code solutions, whereas companies desiring full control may lean towards bespoke or component-based solutions. Open-source solutions may be suited to both scenarios.

4 BESPOKE DEVELOPMENT

INTRODUCTION

In the previous chapter, bespoke development was discussed as one of a number of options for acquiring a digital solution. This referred to an approach where organisations build software from scratch, either using in-house teams or by commissioning an external development organisation to build the software on their behalf. However, all software needs to be developed at some point, so, even though a software vendor may be developing a software package that they intend to sell, or a collaborative team of developers is creating software that it subsequently offers on an open-source basis, the software must be developed to meet a set of requirements.

This chapter explores how development teams organise and manage the process of developing software to meet a set of requirements. Book 3 in this series, *Delivering Digital Solutions*, considers **software engineering** in terms of the more technical aspects of creating software.

DEFINED VERSUS EMPIRICAL APPROACHES

With bespoke development, the solution is built from scratch to precisely realise an agreed set of requirements. Acceptance of the end solution is dependent on it exactly meeting these agreed requirements.

Bespoke approaches typically fall into one of two categories: defined or empirical. These approaches cover how to organise the work of the development project. They do not define how to write good software, which is explored in *Delivering Digital Solutions*. A high-level comparison of the key features of each approach is provided in Table 4.1.

Table 4.1 Defined and empirical approaches

Defined	Empirical
Linear life cycle	Iterative life cycle
Requirements defined and baselined up-front	Requirements evolve throughout the project
Requirements prioritised up-front	Requirements reprioritised throughout the project

(Continued)

Table 4.1 (Continued)

Defined	Empirical
Complete solution developed prior to delivery	Solution developed iteratively
Single solution delivered at the end of the project	Solution delivered incrementally throughout the project
Copes poorly with change	Adaptive to change
Documentation-intensive	Just enough documentation, just in time
Focuses on deliverables and project milestones	Focuses on regular delivery of valuable working software
Managed teams	Self-organising teams
Siloed roles	Collaboration
Delivers what was signed off	Delivers a fit-for-purpose solution

Defined approaches

Defined approaches are based on the premise that it is desirable to define a simple, repeatable process, or set of processes, supported by a set of standard templates and techniques, to produce consistent project deliverables, and in doing so, the project team will be able to deliver a predictable outcome.

This approach is based around a linear, sequential framework, as follows:

1. The solution requirements are defined, agreed and typically signed off and baselined.

2. The requirements form the basis of a design specification that shows how they are to be realised.

3. The software (program code) is then written in accordance with the design specification.

4. The software undergoes a series of tests to ensure it works correctly, in line with the design specification and requirements.

5. The final step is for the tested solution to be deployed into a production environment for live operational use.

Defined approaches are characterised by the following key features:

Linear life cycle	Projects are split into stages where each is completed and signed off prior to the next stage commencing.
Requirements defined and baselined up-front	Comprehensive requirements are defined, baselined and signed off before solution design and development commences.

Requirements prioritised up-front	Priorities are agreed for each requirement prior to baselining and sign-off. These constrain the development and delivery of solution features and any changes to the priorities are subject to a change control process.
Complete solution developed prior to delivery	Once prioritised, baselined and signed off, the complete set of requirements is handed over to the development team, who designs, builds and tests a solution to fully realise these requirements with little, if any, feedback from the customer or end-users until the final acceptance testing stage.
Single solution delivered at the end of the project	The customer and end-users do not receive anything of any real value until the end of the project, when the entire solution is deployed for live operational use. If the project is abandoned mid-way, there is no real value to the business.
Copes poorly with change	Since key deliverables are signed off and baselined at the end of each stage of the project, any subsequent changes are subject to a formal change control process, which can involve significant re-work of previously signed-off deliverables. This often leads to a tendency to resist making changes (even if they are beneficial to the organisation) or to defer them to a subsequent development project.
Documentation-intensive	The need to define and sign-off a comprehensive set of requirements prior to design and development results in a large amount of documentation being generated up-front. This ensures there is agreement between the customer and the development team early in the project around exactly what needs to be built, before committing significant resources to building the solution. However, this also incurs a significant elapsed time before software development work commences, and often results in the documentation becoming out of date and subject to remedial work to keep it up to date.
Focuses on deliverables and project milestones	For projects with a significant elapsed time between the sign-off and baselining of the customer requirements and the completion of the solution, by the time the customer and end-users are re-engaged to undertake acceptance testing, the solution may no longer be fit for purpose.

Managed teams	Defined approaches often lead to increased levels of bureaucracy and teams being micro-managed, whereby a project manager is constantly checking that the team members are working according to predefined targets and milestones. This phenomenon is eloquently articulated by Dr Stephen Covey (2020):

> You cannot hold people responsible for results if you supervise their methods. You then become responsible for results and rules replace human judgement, creativity, responsibility.

Siloed roles	The formality and reliance upon signed off documentation can lead to project actors[1] working independently of each other, relying on documentation-based deliverables as a main form of communication, rather than actively collaborating.
Delivers what was signed off	See explanation under *Focuses on deliverables and project milestones* above.

Common criticisms aimed at projects based around this approach are:

- They run over time and budget.[2]
- They do not cope well with changes after requirements have been baselined.
- Practitioners follow the processes blindly, without considering the reasons why they should be carried out, or if they are necessary or valuable.
- Increased levels of documentation – which can become out of date – lead to increased bureaucracy.
- The solution fails to fully meet the business need due to lack of customer/user feedback.

Empirical approaches

In contrast to defined approaches, empirical approaches to digital solution development are based on the premise that:

- knowledge comes from experience and making decisions based on what is known;
- requirements are not well understood, or cannot be well articulated, early in the development life cycle;

---

1 An actor is a stakeholder with an active role to play.

2 While this is true for all software projects irrespective of the method (because the deep understanding of the problem space only emerges as the project progresses), an iterative approach may allow the project to offer some value before rising costs call a halt to the work.

- early and continuous feedback from customers/end-users is essential to ensure that a fit-for-purpose solution is delivered; and

- early delivery is more important than completeness.

To support this philosophy, empirical approaches are underpinned by three foundational pillars: transparency, inspection and adaptation (Figure 4.1).

Figure 4.1 The three pillars of an empirical approach

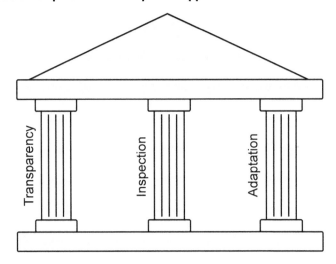

| Transparency | Transparency means that the work of the project team (both good and bad) is available for all to see, and stakeholders responsible for the outcomes of the project have visibility of the process they are following and an understanding of what they are seeing, which leads to a greater sense of ownership. |

Active user involvement and a cooperative, collaborative approach to the development of the solution provide excellent visibility for key stakeholders, both of the project's progress and of the product itself, which in turn helps to ensure that expectations are effectively managed.

| Inspection | Frequent inspection of the product under development and the progress to-date allows the project team to see what it has done well and where it needs to improve. |

Key stakeholders frequently inspect the artefacts produced during the project, and progress towards a goal, to detect undesirable variances and provide feedback that can be used to adapt the process, or incrementally improve the artefact, in readiness for the next inspection.

Adaptation

During inspection, if it is determined that one or more aspects of a process or artefact deviates from acceptable limits, and that the resulting product will be unacceptable, the process or the artefact must be adjusted. An adjustment must be made as soon as possible to minimise further deviation.

In empirical projects, change is expected. Requirements emerge and evolve as the product is developed. Code is refactored to adapt to new ideas uncovered through feedback from inspections.

Empirical approaches have grown in popularity over the past two decades due to several factors:

- There are new commercial pressures to obtain a competitive advantage by deploying a digital solution more quickly.

- Business changes are taking place at an ever-increasing rate and require solutions that keep up with the pace of change.

- Technology continues to change at a fast rate and user expectations of digital solutions are increasing, requiring a more feature-driven approach.

- Applications developed using defined methodologies have historically taken so long to build that requirements changed before the development was complete, resulting in inadequate or even unusable solutions.

- The promise of defined methodologies, that a single requirements stage at the beginning of the project would identify all the critical requirements, has been proved to be unrealistic.

Empirical approaches are characterised by the following key features:

Iterative life cycle

Projects are split into a series of timeboxed developments called iterations or Sprints.[3] Each iteration has a predetermined goal (typically articulated in terms of what a user will be able to do using the working software developed during the iteration). In this way, empirical projects are essentially made up of a series of mini-projects, each leading to the development of a partial working solution.

Requirements evolve throughout the project

Requirements will come to light and be elaborated and refined as the project progresses, rather than a comprehensive set of requirements being defined, baselined and signed off at the beginning of the project.

Requirements reprioritised throughout the project

Since requirements evolve throughout the project, they must be continually prioritised and reprioritised as the project progresses, to ensure that the project team works on delivering the most important requirements at any given time.

---

3 Sprint is the name used to refer to an iteration by the Scrum Agile development method. From herein the term iteration shall be used, but the two terms are essentially synonymous.

Solution developed iteratively	Given that early and continuous feedback from customers/end-users is essential to ensure that a fit-for-purpose solution is delivered, the project team must develop something that works as soon as possible, so that the customer/end-users can provide feedback to the project team, who can then refine the product while adding further features during the next iteration.
Solution delivered incrementally throughout the project	Another premise underpinning empirical approaches is that early delivery is more important than completeness. It is more valuable to the customer/end-users to have a partial solution that can be used early on to realise business benefits, rather than wait for a complete solution at the end of the project.
Adaptive to change	As requirements are not baselined and signed off early in the project, new requirements or changes to existing requirements arising later can simply be added to the solution backlog and reprioritised at the start of the next development iteration.
Just enough documentation, just in time	A common criticism of defined approaches is that they are too documentation-intensive. In contrast, the philosophy behind empirical approaches is 'just enough, just in time'. Therefore, documentation is only produced when and where it adds value.
Focuses on regular delivery of valuable working software	The value from digital solution development is realised through the use of the solution in support of the relevant business objectives. There is little direct value to the business in the documentation produced during the solution development process. Empirical approaches therefore focus on the development and delivery of working software, and only produce documentation where it is essential to achieve this, or where the documentation has other beneficial uses.
Self-organising teams	Empirical approaches employ feedback mechanisms to monitor and adapt to the unexpected, providing regularity and predictability. Less time is spent planning and defining tasks and creating and reading documentation; more time is spent understanding what is happening and responding. Team members empirically devise and execute the best processes possible based on their skills, experience and the situation in which they find themselves.
Collaboration	By involving business stakeholders at the beginning and end of every iteration, the project team understands what the business stakeholders need and creates a solution that meets that need, refining the solution as the project proceeds based on regular feedback from the business stakeholders, to ensure that the end solution is fit for purpose.
Delivers a fit-for-purpose solution	As a result of collaborating closely with business stakeholders, the end solution is more likely to be a closer fit to the business need.

SOFTWARE DEVELOPMENT LIFE CYCLES

A software development life cycle (SDLC) is a framework that the selected development approach is built upon. Defined approaches are based on linear life cycles, such as the Waterfall life cycle or the 'V' model life cycle, whereas empirical approaches are based on iterative life cycles. The most popular life cycles are described below.

The Waterfall life cycle

Winston W. Royce (1970), an American computer scientist and director of Lockheed Software Technology Centre in Austin, Texas at the time, is generally considered to be the father of the SDLC, and in particular the Waterfall life cycle.

The main feature of the Waterfall life cycle is that the development project is divided into a number of discrete stages, each representing a significant portion of the development work. Each stage in the life cycle must be completed (and some deliverable signed off) before the next stage can commence.

Figure 4.2 provides a more current re-working of the Waterfall life cycle that includes the practice of Requirements Engineering, which had not been devised at the time of Royce's paper.

Figure 4.2 Waterfall development life cycle

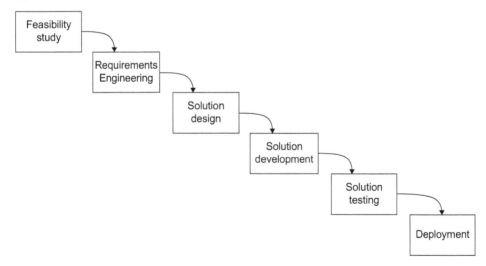

Feasibility study

This is a short study that identifies the high-level business requirements for a solution development project and considers a range of options for realising them. There are three aspects of feasibility considered: business, technical and financial. The main deliverable is a business case with recommendations. A feasibility study enables the decision-makers to determine whether it is worth investing in the project.

Requirements Engineering

This stage (referred to as analysis in Figure 1.1) involves investigating the solution requirements in detail. The deliverable is usually a comprehensive specification of what is required in the form of a Business Requirements Document (BRD – see Chapter 5).

Solution design

In this stage, the BRD is translated into a technical design capable of being implemented using the proposed hardware and software platforms. The main deliverable is a set of solution design documentation that specifies how the requirements in the BRD are to be realised.

Solution development

In this stage, working software is created in accordance with the design documentation produced in the previous stage. The main deliverable is the working software ready for solution testing.

Solution testing

This stage comprises a series of different testing activities. Testing starts with unit testing (of the individual programs or components) and progresses to integration testing (checking that the programs work together as intended), then on to system testing (checking that the entire system works as a coherent software product) and, finally, acceptance testing (ensuring that the software product is fit for purpose and meets the business need). The main deliverable is a fully tested working solution ready for deployment into a live operational environment.

Deployment

Finally, once accepted by the business stakeholders, the solution is transferred into a live (production) environment for operational use. This stage also involves the training of relevant stakeholders who will be using or supporting the solution and any necessary data creation and/or migration from other data sources.

The 'V' model life cycle

The 'V' model life cycle is similar to the Waterfall life cycle, in so far as it divides a solution development project into a series of stages, each one being completed and appropriate deliverables signed off prior to the commencement of the next stage. However, it differs from the Waterfall model in two significant ways (see Figure 4.3):

- The number of stages is extended to explicitly identify the different testing activities as separate stages (shown on the right-hand side of the model).

- The early specification stages shown on the left-hand side of the model are linked to corresponding testing stages on the right-hand side of the model.

Figure 4.3 'V' model development life cycle

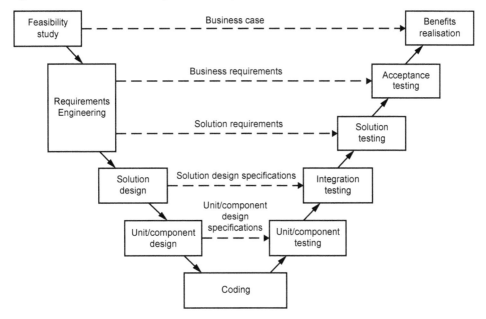

For many years the 'V' model has been the life cycle of choice for the testing community because it focuses on quality assurance throughout the entire SDLC rather than as a single stage at the end of the life cycle. It also makes explicit connections between the early specification stages of a solution development project and the later testing stages, indicating that the deliverables produced during the specification stages form the basis for the corresponding testing stages.

The version of the 'V' model life cycle shown in Figure 4.3 is a reimagining of the original model to show Requirements Engineering explicitly. This version has also been extended to show the feasibility study as the first stage and its connection with benefits realisation, which takes place after the solution has been deployed. Deployment is not shown as a separate stage in its own right in the 'V' model, but essentially takes place between acceptance testing and benefits realisation.

The iterative life cycle

The Waterfall and 'V' model life cycles support defined approaches to solution development and are both based on the assumption that business stakeholders can specify at an early stage what they need the solution to do. The fact that this is often not the case gave rise to empirical approaches supported by an iterative life cycle. An early incarnation of the iterative life cycle was the Spiral Model (Boehm, 1986), although Royce himself did suggest a more iterative approach in his 1970 paper. Figure 4.4 shows a more recent version of the iterative life cycle, although different Agile methods have their own versions.

Figure 4.4 Iterative development life cycle (© Assist Knowledge Development Ltd)

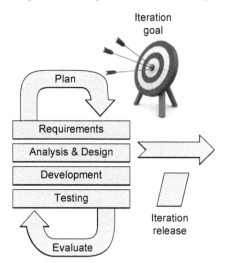

Iterative development is based around a **solution backlog** of high-level requirements, which are typically generated outside the iteration. Figure 4.4 shows the key activities involved within each iteration.

Planning	A planning session is held at the start of each iteration, during which the development team agrees with the business owner (also referred to as the product owner) the requirements from the solution backlog that shall be developed into working software during the iteration. This subset of requirements forms the **iteration backlog**, from which a detailed plan for carrying out the development work is agreed.
Requirements	High-level requirements are typically captured as user stories, which are stored in the solution backlog for subsequent refinement, prioritisation and estimation. Prioritisation and estimation typically take place as part of iteration planning, resulting in the formation of the iteration backlog, but refinement often takes place before the iteration begins.
Analysis and design	Analysis is undertaken by BAs and involves elaborating iteration backlog items to ensure that there is sufficient clarity to enable a developer to design and build each feature as working software. Techniques such as scenario analysis and prototyping are used to explore ways of meeting the requirements within the iteration backlog and to check and resolve the business and technical issues associated with them.
	Design is undertaken by the developer, often in conjunction with user experience (UX) designers and solution architects, and involves making decisions about how the requirements will be translated into working software.

Development and testing	Development involves writing program code (also known as source code) and using a set of tools such as an integrated development environment (IDE) and continuous integration and continuous delivery (CI/CD) pipelines to translate that into executable software.

Development and testing are often combined, with the developer undertaking unit testing (also known as program, component or module testing) while refining the source code, although specialist testing (such as stress testing and penetration testing) is conducted as a separate activity. In some cases, the developers will adopt a test-first approach (also known as test-driven development (TDD)) whereby the developer writes tests (which initially fail because there is no program code to execute) before writing the source code. These tests establish strong success criteria for the source code (the failing tests should start passing as the code evolves). TDD is covered in *Delivering Digital Solutions*.

At the conclusion of this work, a potentially deployable solution is made ready to be placed into live operation and released to the user community.

Evaluation	At the end of each iteration the working software is evaluated by the product owner in a session known as a 'show and tell' or 'iteration/Sprint review'. The developers showcase the new functionality that has been developed during the iteration and the product owner confirms whether the working software has met the goal set for the iteration during iteration planning, and whether each element of functionality is fit for purpose.

Following on from the iteration review session, it is commonplace for the team to hold a 'retrospective', where they review how the iteration has gone and identify any improvements that they can make to their working practices.

Iteration release	The release of the working software at the end of the iteration is initially an internal release for demonstration to the product owner during the iteration review session. If the product owner deems the iteration release to be fit for purpose, then they may authorise a deployment into a production environment for live operational use. This is known as 'release when ready'. Sometimes, however, there is a more structured approach to release, with a separate release planning session and the release is made at the end of a predetermined number of iterations, as shown in Figure 4.5.

Where an iterative life cycle forms the basis of the development approach, the solution emerges through the construction of a series of evolutionary prototypes during a number of fixed time (timeboxed) development iterations, each one adding new or enhanced functionality, or improved performance. At the end of each iteration, the final version of the prototype is a potentially deployable working software increment (shown in Figure 4.4 as **iteration release**). The full solution develops over time as the users' and developers' understanding of what is required, and how best to deliver the requirements, grows.

A deployment into live operational use may or may not take place at the end of an iteration and it is common for a series of development iterations to be completed before each release, as shown in Figure 4.5.

More detail regarding how the iterative life cycle works in practice is given in Chapter 6.

Comparison of life cycle models

Table 4.2 Provides a summary of the advantages and disadvantages of the three life cycle models considered above.

Table 4.2 Comparison of SDLC models

Life cycle	Advantages	Disadvantages
Waterfall	• Relatively easy to manage (compared with 'V' model and iterative life cycles) • Good project control and governance • Less duplication of effort	• Low user input • All costs up-front • No benefits until end of project • Doesn't cope with changes
'V' model	*As Waterfall plus ...* • Quality assurance of the solution is considered during each stage	*As Waterfall plus ...* • Additional overhead of testing activities
Iterative	• Best-fit solution due to continuous collaboration with business stakeholders • Regular delivery of features (early benefits) • Responsive to changes • High user input and buy-in (regular feedback and continuous improvement)	• Potential for re-work (as requirements and design evolve) • Potential for scope creep (if not properly managed) • Lack of visibility of the overall solution during the early stages of development

CHOOSING AN APPROACH

When deciding on a solution development approach, there are several key questions to consider:

1. Does the customer expect a complete, fully functional solution before they are prepared to transition to a new way of working, or is an incremental delivery approach acceptable?

2. What skills and expertise exist within the project team?

Figure 4.5 Iterations and releases (© Assist Knowledge Development Ltd)

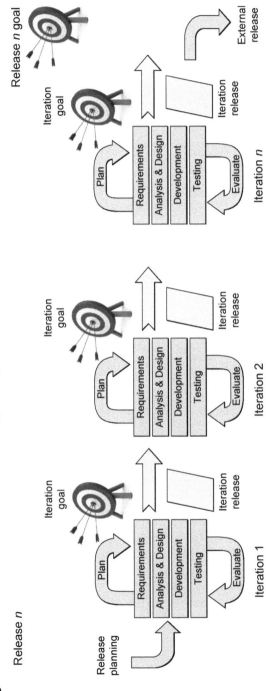

3. Are the project team and key stakeholders in the same location?

4. Is the nature of the required solution safety-critical, user-centric or processing-centric?

5. Does the customer need a high degree of governance, such as traceability, to comply with legislation or regulations?

6. Does the target technical environment impose constraints upon the solution, such as integration with legacy systems, proprietary technologies, text-based versus graphical user interfaces?

7. Are the requirements well known or unclear?

8. Are the requirements relatively independent of each other?

9. Does the organisation have existing standards that govern what deliverables are required to be signed off and when?

10. Is there a culture of trust or a need for accountability, such as exists where there is a contractual relationship with a supplier?

Many of the questions above relate to contextual issues.

- **Q1**: If the answer to question 1 is yes, then a defined approach based around a linear life cycle would seem appropriate, although an empirical approach with a single deployment to production at the end of the project may also be appropriate.

- **Q2**: A lack of understanding of, or experience using, empirical approaches may mean the project team falls back on traditional (defined) approaches that have been successful in the past.

- **Q3**: It is generally accepted that for empirical approaches based around an iterative life cycle to be successful, the project team and key stakeholders should ideally be co-located, although, following COVID-19, organisations have discovered many ways to collaborate without co-location.

- **Q4–6**: The 'V' model life cycle is often seen as the life cycle of choice for safety-critical solutions or solutions requiring a high degree of governance, because of the need for legislative or regulatory compliance. This is due to its focus on quality and testing throughout the development process and the associated traceability and governance that this brings. Defined approaches are often considered the most appropriate where a high degree of processing, especially complex processes, are involved. In contrast, empirical approaches with a high degree of collaboration and user feedback are generally accepted to be most suited to user-centric solutions.

- **Q7**: Where requirements are unclear at the outset of the project, or where there is a degree of technical risk due to the use of new technologies, or technologies not previously used by the project team, an empirical approach is generally more suitable, due to its exploratory nature.

- **Q8**: In theory, the degree of independence between requirements could lead to any approach, but iterative approaches that 'divide and conquer' a large set of requirements and deliver subsets of features through a series of iterations work best when the requirements are relatively independent of each other. Where there is a high degree of dependence between the requirements, the only practical approach may be to deliver a single, complete solution at the end of the project, and therefore a linear approach would be appropriate.

- **Q9**: Empirical approaches, by their nature, tend towards less (or less formal) documentation. Some Agile approaches (discussed in the next section) promote the idea of the code and test cases forming the bulk of the documentation. This may be workable if the development team is permanently assigned to the solution until it is decommissioned, and therefore have a high degree of familiarity with the codebase; however, the idea that someone can read 100,000 lines of code to understand the design and intent of a software component is unrealistic, at best.

- **Q10**: The reduction in formality and less extensive documentation discussed above may present problems where a formal contractual relationship exists, or where there is a culture based on a lack of trust. In this situation a defined approach based on a linear life cycle that incorporates formal sign-off of artefacts during each stage may be necessary.

AGILE SOFTWARE DEVELOPMENT

Defined and empirical approaches to bespoke software development were introduced earlier in this chapter. Starting around the early 1990s, empirical approaches became increasingly popular as a response to the failings of the more 'heavyweight' defined methods, which had dominated the software development industry following the introduction of the Waterfall SDLC in 1970. This culminated in a meeting of minds in February 2001, which led to the formation of the **Agile Manifesto** (discussed below).

Agile software development is a set of practices and methodologies that align to the Agile Manifesto and embrace the Agile philosophy, prioritising responding to changes and delivering working software that offers value to customers, quickly and frequently.

The Agile philosophy

It is often said that an essential component for successful Agile software development is an **Agile mindset** that fully embraces the **Agile philosophy**. The Agile mindset refers to the set of attitudes, beliefs and ways of thinking that embody the principles of the Agile approach, as defined in the Agile Manifesto, and focuses on a way of working that values flexibility, adaptability, collaboration and continuous improvement. The Agile philosophy refers to the broader, overarching framework of values and principles that guide Agile methodologies, which is rooted in the Agile Manifesto.

The Agile Manifesto

In February 2001, a group of software development practitioners came together to discuss better ways of developing software. The output from this meeting was published as the Agile Manifesto (Beck et al., 2001), and they formed an organisation called the Agile Alliance to maintain and promote Agile ways of working. The publication of the Agile Manifesto led to the adoption of the term 'Agile', first within software development circles and later more widely within organisations seeking to become more 'Agile'.

For the purposes of this book, Agile is an umbrella term used to categorise a series of 'lightweight' software development methods that align themselves to the Agile Manifesto, and are underpinned by the three pillars of an empirical approach introduced earlier in this chapter.

The Agile Manifesto is not a method, a process or a set of techniques; it is a set of four values underpinned by 12 principles.

Agile values
The four values from the Agile Manifesto are shown in Figure 4.6.

Figure 4.6 The Agile Manifesto values

We are uncovering better ways of developing software by doing it and helping others do it. Through this work we have come to value:

Individuals and interactions *over* **processes and tools**
Working software *over* **comprehensive documentation**
Customer collaboration *over* **contract negotiation**
Responding to change *over* **following a plan**

That is, while there is value in the items on the right, we value the items on the left more.

Agile principles
In addition to the four key values, the Agile Manifesto is underpinned by 12 core principles:

1. Our highest priority is to satisfy the customer through early and continuous delivery of valuable software.

2. Welcome changing requirements, even late in development. Agile processes harness change for the customer's competitive advantage.

3. Deliver working software frequently, from a couple of weeks to a couple of months, with preference to the shorter timescale.

4. Business people and developers must work together daily throughout the project.

5. Build projects around motivated individuals. Give them the environment and support they need, and trust them to get the job done.

6. The most efficient and effective method of conveying information to and within a development team is face-to-face conversation.

7. Working software is the primary measure of progress.

8. Agile processes promote sustainable development. The sponsors, developers and users should be able to maintain a constant pace indefinitely.

9. Continuous attention to technical excellence and good design enhances agility.

10. Simplicity – the art of maximising the amount of work not done – is essential.

11. The best architectures, requirements and designs emerge from self-organising teams.

12. At regular intervals, the team reflects on how to become more effective, then tunes and adjusts its behaviour accordingly.

Popular Agile methods

In general terms, a method provides guidance to help achieve a particular outcome in a predictable and repeatable way. It can take the form of a list of actions or steps that assist in the delivery of the outcome. In the context of digital solution development, a method tends to be based around one of the SDLC models introduced earlier in this chapter. Some methods are more prescriptive than others and also mandate specific roles and responsibilities, deliverables, techniques and standards. Figure 4.7 provides an overview of the various elements incorporated within a software development method.

Figure 4.7 Elements of a software development method

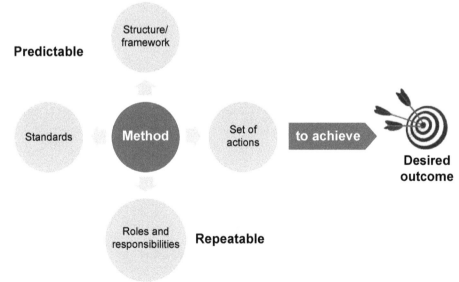

Agile methods are often described as 'lightweight' because, compared to their 'defined' predecessors, they are less prescriptive. A detailed comparison of Agile methods is beyond the scope of this book, so this section focuses on introducing the key features of the most popular methods at the time of writing (December 2024).

Scrum

Commonly described as simple, elegant and empirical (guided by experience), Scrum is based on a set of common-sense guidelines for managing the work required to develop a product, rather than being based on a project life cycle. The team adapts its approach based on experience rather than following a rigorous set of steps or a very detailed plan.

The word Scrum itself comes from the game of rugby football and refers to a way of restarting the game after an infringement. In the software development method, the **Scrum** refers to a daily stand-up meeting that essentially 'kicks-off' the work for the day.

Scrum achieves significantly increased productivity with reduced time to benefits realisation, with a relatively straightforward implementation, by focusing the Scrum Team on producing a potentially shippable product at the end of every **Sprint**. Sprint (synonymous with iteration) is the name for a fixed time period referred to as a **timebox** (discussed later in this chapter) during which a potentially releasable product increment is developed to achieve a product goal determined by the product owner. The length of a Sprint can vary from project to project, or even from team to team, and typically ranges from one week to one month.

Figure 4.8 shows an overview of the mechanics of the Scrum method.

Figure 4.8 Overview of the Scrum method

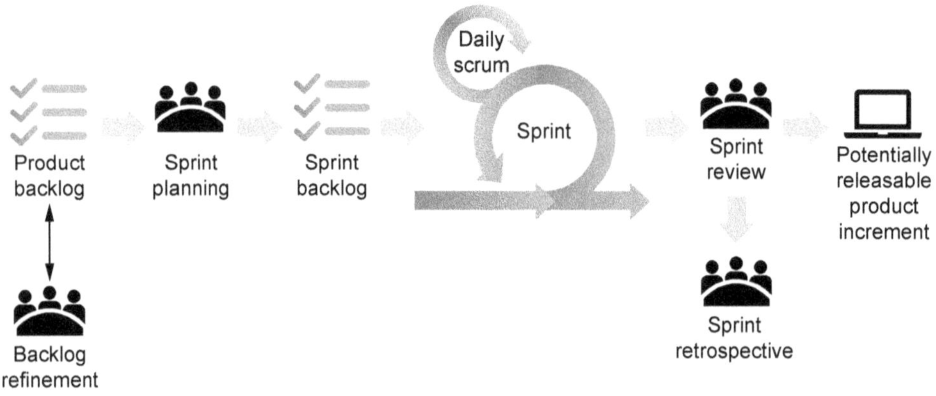

The Scrum process starts with a **product backlog**, which comprises a set of requirements for the product to be developed, created by the **product owner**. The product owner is one of only three roles defined in the Scrum Guide (Schwaber and Sutherland, 2020), the others being the **Scrum Master** and **developer**. The product owner is 'accountable for maximising the value of the product resulting from the work of the Scrum Team'. The Scrum Master is 'accountable for the Scrum Team's effectiveness', and developers are the people in the Scrum Team that are committed to creating any aspect of a usable increment in each Sprint.

Scrum defines a series of events (often referred to as **ceremonies**). These ceremonies (see later in this chapter) have been widely adopted by Agile development teams, regardless of whether they employ Scrum as a method.

Extreme Programming

Extreme Programming (or 'XP' as its proponents refer to it) evolved as an extreme version of an earlier empirical method called Rapid Application Development (RAD). It has been described by Jeffries et al. (2001) as:

> ... a discipline of software development with values of simplicity, communication, feedback and courage ... [that focus] on the roles of customer, manager, and programmer and accord key rights and responsibilities to the people in those roles.

XP is a product-based method, whereby a relatively small team builds a single software product, adopting similar controls and ceremonies to Scrum, with three significant additions:

Architectural spike	XP projects typically start with a set of user stories (akin to the product backlog in Scrum) and an architectural spike. The latter is a technical risk-reduction technique where just enough code is written to explore the use of an unfamiliar technology or technique. This results in a simple overall design known as the system metaphor.
Spike	A spike is a piece of work (typically the development of a simple program) to explore a potential solution to a requirement in order to determine how much work will be required.
Release planning	The most significant difference between Scrum and XP is that Scrum adopts a release-when-ready approach, where the working software produced by the team is deployed when the team (including the product owner) determine that it is ready for release. XP has a separate release planning cycle where the customer determines which features should be included in the next release, and a number of development iterations are completed to build those features.

Unlike Scrum, XP provides further guidance on how to actually build the working software, with practices such as pair programming (developers work in pairs, at the same computer, checking and testing each other's work) and test-first development (writing unit tests before writing the program code and keeping all of the tests running at all times).

Kanban

Kanban is a Japanese term meaning 'signboard' or 'visual signal'. Kanban, the Agile development method, involves a set of practices originally developed as part of the Toyota Production System to improve efficiency on factory floors.

In a Kanban approach, there is less emphasis on up-front iteration planning, as with Scrum and XP. Instead of defined iteration goals, a team usually works from a prioritised backlog and focuses on visualising progress and identifying blockers. This approach trades up-front communication of goals against optimised productivity.

Kanban is based on the following principles:

Visualise the workflow	The core concept of Kanban is to create a visual representation of the entire process using a Kanban board. This board typically includes columns representing different stages of work (such as *To Do*, *In Progress* and *Done* – or, in software development terms, *Backlog*, *In Development*, *In Testing* and *Done*). Each task or item is represented by a card on the board, allowing the team to see the status of work at a glance.
Limit work in progress (WIP)	Kanban emphasises limiting the amount of work in progress at any given time. By setting WIP limits for each stage of the process, teams can focus on finishing tasks before starting new ones, which helps to reduce context switching, prevents bottlenecks and ensures a smoother flow of work. For example, a team may set a WIP limit of three for the *In Development* column, meaning only three tasks can be in progress at a time.
Manage flow	Kanban aims to create a steady and predictable flow of work through the development process. Teams continuously monitor their process and look for ways to optimise it. Metrics such as cycle time and lead time are often tracked to assess performance and identify areas for improvement. For example, if the team notices that tasks are frequently stuck in the *In Testing* column, they may investigate the cause and make adjustments to improve the flow.
Make process policies explicit	The process rules and policies should be clearly defined and communicated to all team members. This helps to ensure that everyone understands how work should be managed and what is expected at each stage. For example, the team might have a policy that no new tasks can enter the *In Development* column until one is moved to *In Testing*.

Implement feedback loops	Regular feedback loops, such as daily stand-ups and retrospectives (see *Agile ceremonies* later in this chapter), help teams to review their progress, discuss any issues and make adjustments to the process. For example, a daily stand-up meeting may involve reviewing the Kanban board and discussing any tasks that are blocked or delayed.
Improve collaboratively, evolve experimentally	Kanban encourages a culture of continuous improvement. Teams regularly reflect on their processes, experiment with changes and adopt what works best. For example, the team may decide to try a new WIP limit or add a *Code Review* column based on feedback from the retrospective.

Kanban can be combined with Scrum, when it is referred to as ScrumBan.

DSDM Agile Project Framework

Both Scrum and XP focus on the development and continuous evolution of a software product, and, while they can be undertaken within a project context, they do not define any project-specific elements. The DSDM (Dynamic Systems Development Method) Agile Project Framework, developed by a consortium of user and vendor organisations, on the other hand, is an Agile method aimed at larger Agile development projects.

The DSDM Agile Project Framework defines 13 roles with specific responsibilities and the work is structured around a life cycle composed of four key project stages, in addition to a pre-project and a post-project stage:

Pre-project	The pre-project stage is often referred to as 'discovery' in the business analysis community. It involves investigating a business situation and formalising a proposal for a digital solution development project.
Feasibility	The project team decides whether a proposed project is viable, typically by producing a business case to evaluate alternative options in terms of costs, benefits, business impact and risks.
Foundations	Firm and enduring foundations are established for the project, by defining terms of reference and establishing an initial solution backlog.
Evolutionary development	DSDM is a project framework that is agnostic on the approach to development, so provides no specific guidance or structure for this stage. This means another method that supports evolutionary development (e.g. Scrum or XP) would typically be adopted for this stage.

Deployment   The focus of the deployment stage is on transitioning the solution developed during the evolutionary development stage into live operational use or preparing for market. This stage has three sequential steps:

1. **Assembly**: Incremental assembly of the solution delivered by one or more solution development teams.

2. **Review**: A final acceptance check is undertaken and the formal decision to deploy the solution into live operational use is made. This stage also incorporates a retrospective of the completed product increment.

3. **Deployment**: The physical deployment of the solution into a production environment ready for full operational use.

Post-project   After the last planned deployment, a reflective review of project performance in terms of business value achieved is conducted.

Lean Software Development

Lean Software Development (LSD) was introduced by Mary and Tom Poppendieck in their book *Lean Software Development: An Agile Toolkit* (Poppendieck and Poppendieck, 2003). It translates lean manufacturing (a set of techniques and tools for eliminating waste and improving productivity in manufacturing) into equivalent practices for software development.

The lean manufacturing system focuses on the elimination of waste and considers the expenditure of resources for any purpose other than the creation of value for the end customer as waste. Agile development practices seek to eliminate waste but, to do this, it is first necessary to *see* the waste. If something does not directly add value, as perceived by the customer, it is waste.

There are seven key lean practices upon which LSD is based. From these key practices, the Poppendiecks devised a set of tools. Table 4.3 shows the mapping of the LSD tools to lean practices.

Shigeo Shingo, one of the originators of the Toyota Production System, identified seven types of manufacturing waste (although modern Lean practitioners now recognise eight). The Poppendiecks compared these types of waste to their equivalents in software development. Table 4.4 shows the mapping between manufacturing and software development wastes.

LSD does not focus on describing how to develop software. Consequently, it is typically combined with other approaches such as Scrum, XP and Kanban.

Table 4.3 Mapping of LSD tools to lean practices

Lean practice	LSD tool
Eliminate waste	• Seeing waste • Value stream mapping
Amplify learning	• Feedback • Iterations • Synchronisation • Set-based development
Decide as late as possible	• Options thinking • The last responsible moment • Making decisions
Deliver as fast as possible	• Pull systems • Queuing theory • Cost of delay
Empower the team	• Self-determination • Motivation • Leadership • Expertise
Build integrity in	• Perceived integrity • Conceptual integrity • Refactoring • Testing
See the whole	• Measurements • Contracts

Table 4.4 Manufacturing wastes versus software development wastes

Manufacturing waste	Software development equivalent
Inventory	Partially done work
Extra processing	Extra processes
Overproduction	Extra features
Transportation	Task switching
Waiting	Waiting
Motion	Motion
Defects	Defects

Scaled Agile Framework®

The Scaled Agile Framework (SAFe®) is a system for scaling Agile across teams, business units and even entire organisations.

According to its creator, Dean Leffingwell (Scaled Agile, Inc., 2023), SAFe, which was at version 6.0 at the time of writing (December 2024), is:

> a knowledge base of proven, integrated principles, practices, and competencies for achieving business agility using Lean, Agile, and DevOps.

It recognises that large organisations have varying levels of delivery management and that Agile methods, such as Scrum, cannot easily scale to accommodate this.

SAFe is built around seven core competencies of business agility:

- lean Agile leadership;
- team and technical agility;
- Agile product delivery;
- enterprise solution delivery;
- lean portfolio management;
- organisational agility; and
- continuous learning culture.

SAFe can be applied in different configurations, including essential, large solution and portfolio. A key concept within SAFe is the Agile Release Train, which enables the outputs of a number of different development teams to be coordinated into a continuous delivery pipeline.

COMMON AGILE PRACTICES AND TECHNIQUES

Agile practices and techniques are specific concepts and activities used by teams to help them embrace the Agile mindset and implement Agile methodologies effectively, in order to deliver software incrementally and adapt to changes quickly. Some of the most common Agile practices are described below.

Backlogs

The concept of a backlog is fundamental to Agile development methods as it forms a repository for the requirements associated with the development of a software product.

Scrum was introduced earlier in this chapter as an Agile method that uses two backlogs: the **product backlog** and the **Sprint backlog**, as shown in Figure 4.8. The product backlog (more generically known as the **solution backlog**) is the master backlog containing all requirements for the product under development, while the Sprint backlog (more generically known as the **iteration backlog**) contains just the items to be developed into working software during the current Sprint (iteration); the Sprint backlog is the main output from Sprint planning.

In some Agile teams the backlog is ordered, with the most important item being placed at the top, so that the development team can simply work through the items in order. An alternative is to use a separate prioritisation system like MoSCoW (described below), which was popularised in DSDM.

In some methods (e.g. XP) where there is a built-in release cycle, a third backlog is used: the **release backlog**. In this case, the release backlog is a subset of the solution backlog that contains only those items planned for release in the next incremental deployment of the software product, and the iteration backlog is a subset of the release backlog.

Backlogs are explored further in Chapter 6.

Timeboxing

Timeboxing is a practice for controlling activities and tasks by allocating a fixed, limited amount of time to the task or activity. This ensures focus and timely progress, and prevents tasks from expanding unnecessarily. Working in a timebox encourages the team or individual working on the task or activity to determine what work or artefact is most important to complete within the time frame, so that this is worked on first, in case there is insufficient time to complete everything that was planned for the timebox.

The use of timeboxes for development iterations has led to the adoption of the concept of a **minimum viable product** (MVP) to ensure the team produces something viable that works during each iteration.

The timeboxed development iterations create a predictable structure for development to progress and ensure that new features are completed and delivered in regular increments – typically every two weeks, although some development teams work to one-week, three-week, four-week or even six-week timeboxes. In addition to iterations, timeboxes are also used for Agile ceremonies (described later in this chapter). For example, according to the Scrum Guide, the daily Scrums (daily stand-up meetings) are timeboxed to 15 minutes. Other tasks and activities such as workshops can also be timeboxed to maintain focus.

Timeboxing encourages prioritisation to ensure the maximum benefit is derived within the limited time frame. The MoSCoW prioritisation system (described later in this chapter) works particularly well with iteration and release timeboxes to determine which backlog items can be developed or delivered during the timebox. This is discussed further in Chapter 6.

Iterative development

Iterative development refers to how software is built, based on the iterative SDLC, whereby a development project is composed of several small, timeboxed developments (iterations/Sprints), which take place in sequence. Each iteration is essentially a self-contained mini-project composed of activities such as requirements, analysis, design, development and testing, as visualised in Figure 4.4.

With iterative development, the solution emerges through the construction of a series of evolutionary prototypes over a series of development iterations, each adding new or enhanced functionality, improved performance or fixes for defects introduced earlier in development. At the end of each iteration, the final version of the prototype is a working, potentially deployable piece of software (shown in Figure 4.4 as the iteration release). The full solution evolves over time as the users' and developers' understanding of what is required, and how best to deliver the requirements, grows.

A deployment into live operational use may or may not take place at the end of an iteration (see *Incremental delivery* below) and it is common for a series of development iterations to be completed before deploying the software into a production environment, as shown in Figure 4.5.

Incremental delivery

Incremental delivery is typically combined with iterative development. Traditional approaches, based on linear SDLCs, deliver a complete solution at the end of a development project. However, this all-or-nothing approach is not workable for many modern businesses because it requires a large up-front investment with no benefits being realised until the project is complete. This means that if a project is abandoned before it is complete, the business has invested often significant resources in the project with no real value being achieved. To mitigate this risk, development teams in the 1990s started to tailor their approach to deliver a partial solution early and then regularly add more features through subsequent 'increments' of the solution. This incremental delivery approach led to earlier realisation of benefits and is now an integral part of Agile development projects.

For incremental delivery to work in practice, it is imperative that the business has workarounds in place to mitigate the impact of the missing product features, and that each release provides a viable product that can be used by the organisation to realise value – the MVP concept was introduced earlier in this chapter and is an important focus during prioritisation and release planning in Agile projects. The MVP concept is also used during iteration planning.

Collaboration

Collaborative working is the ability of two or more individuals, groups or organisations to work closely together. It encourages stakeholders to forge strong working relationships with a focus on a common goal, and leads to improved communication and cooperation, enhancing transparency, alignment and collective ownership of outcomes.

Agile ceremonies (e.g. iteration planning, show and tells and retrospectives) rely on collaboration between the relevant stakeholders, which helps to build trust while requiring less formality and documentation.

Self-organising teams

Teams that manage their own work, make decisions collectively and adapt dynamically to changes without external micromanagement, promote accountability and cultivate innovation. For example, Agile development teams decide how to accomplish iteration goals and distribute tasks among themselves, rather than work being assigned to them by a project manager. These self-organising teams can only be effective where there is a culture of trust and empowerment. To quote Steve Jobs:

> It doesn't make sense to hire smart people and tell them what to do; we hire smart people so they can tell us what to do.

Continuous improvement

Continuous improvement is a core principle in Agile development. Principle 12 from the Agile Manifesto, introduced earlier in this chapter, states:

> At regular intervals, the team reflects on how to become more effective, then tunes and adjusts its behaviour accordingly.

This ensures that teams regularly assess and refine their processes, practices and deliverables, leading to incremental enhancements to their performance and the quality of their outputs.

The most visible continuous improvement practice is the retrospective that takes place at the end of each iteration, but there are other less obvious practices that also contribute to continuous improvement. Some of the most common practices include:

Iteration reviews	Teams review deliverables at the end of each iteration to evaluate progress and ensure alignment with customer needs. This provides an opportunity for stakeholders to give feedback, enabling the team to make refinements during future iterations.
Retrospectives	A retrospective is a meeting that takes place at the end of each iteration (typically immediately following the iteration review), where the team reflects on what went well, what didn't and how to improve. See *Agile ceremonies* below for further details.

Kaizen	The word Kaizen derives from two Japanese words – **Kai**, meaning change, and **zen**, meaning good or better – so it literally translates to **change for the better**. Kaizen focuses on making small, incremental changes often, enabling teams to address inefficiencies and bottlenecks without significant disruptions. Originating from the Toyota Production System, Kaizen has been widely adopted by almost every other type of industry as part of the Lean methodology.
Metrics and feedback loops	Use of quantitative and qualitative metrics (such as velocity, lead time, cycle time and defect rates) to assess performance provides data-driven insights and highlights areas for improvement. For example, if the velocity of a team drops, the team may identify and resolve any blockers.
Peer reviews and pair programming	Peer reviews involve team members reviewing each other's work to suggest quality improvements. **Pair programming** (a practice popularised by the XP Agile method) involves two developers working together on the same task, checking each other's work and spotting potential defects, which are fixed early in the development cycle. Both of these practices encourage knowledge sharing and improve the quality of work.
Customer feedback integration	Regularly engaging with customers or end-users to gather input on product increments ensures that the solution continues to be improved throughout its development.
Experimentation and prototyping	Regular testing of new ideas, technologies or approaches on a small scale promotes innovation while mitigating risks.
Cross-functional collaboration	Regularly improving how developers, testers, designers and business stakeholders work together enhances team alignment and reduces silos.
Tackling technical debt	Proactively addressing suboptimal program code, software architecture or processes that hinder progress leads to improved long-term maintainability and scalability of digital solutions.
Celebrating wins and milestones	Recognising achievements, both big and small, boosts morale, cultivates motivation and reinforces positive behaviours within the team.

Agile ceremonies

Agile ceremonies are structured events that help Agile teams to stay aligned, focused and productive throughout the development process. They are an integral part of Agile methodologies such as Scrum and Kanban, providing a framework for planning, reviewing progress and reflecting on the team's work.

The most popular ceremonies in current use are described below.

Iteration planning	Iteration planning (Sprint planning in Scrum) is the event that initiates an iteration by determining the items from the solution backlog that will be developed during the iteration. Iteration planning results in the creation of the iteration backlog and a plan for the team to complete the necessary work. Iteration planning is typically timeboxed to four hours for a two-week iteration.
Daily stand-up	A daily stand-up meeting (Daily Scrum in Scrum) occurs at the same time each day (typically at the start of the day) within the iteration. Timeboxed to just 15 minutes, the purpose of the meeting is for the team members to inspect progress towards the iteration goal and, where necessary, adapt the iteration backlog and planned work. Any impediments that are preventing the team from progressing with the plan are identified during the daily stand-up and these become the responsibility of the team leader (Scrum Master in Scrum) to resolve.
Iteration review (show and tell)	At the end of the iteration the working software built by the team during the iteration is inspected by the product owner and other relevant stakeholders. The product owner determines whether the iteration goal has been met and any necessary adaptations to the product are identified and added to the solution backlog ready for the next iteration planning session. Additional features may also be identified and added to the solution backlog. Iteration reviews are typically timeboxed to two hours for a two-week iteration.
Retrospective	The retrospective (retro, or Sprint retrospective in Scrum) typically follows directly after the iteration review and provides an opportunity for the team to reflect on the work they have just completed, with a focus on continuous improvement. Retros encourage a culture of learning and adaptability by addressing pain points and celebrating successes. Any helpful suggestions for changes to ways of working (which could include the behaviour of individuals, interactions between team members, processes or use of tools) are actioned in the next iteration. Retrospectives are typically timeboxed to 90 minutes for a two-week iteration.
Backlog refinement	A backlog refinement session (formerly known as backlog grooming) is a collaborative meeting where the solution backlog (or a subset of the backlog) is reviewed to ensure the backlog items (typically in the form of user stories) are clearly defined, prioritised and sized, and are ready for the next iteration planning session. Although not a formal ceremony in Scrum, the Scrum Guide (Schwaber and Sutherland, 2020) suggests that during a Sprint the product backlog is refined as needed.

Backlog refinement sessions can take place between a BA and a developer, a BA and a product owner or a BA, developer and software tester. The latter is often referred to as a **Three Amigos** session and the focus is to ensure that each party correctly understands the requirement encapsulated in the backlog item, and collectively agree a set of **acceptance criteria**, which forms the basis for iteration planning, design, development and testing.

Definition of done

Definition of done (DoD) is a key concept in Agile development. It refers to a shared understanding within an Agile development team of what it means for a task, user story or feature to be considered completely finished (done). It ensures consistent quality and clarity, reducing ambiguity about task completion. An example of DoD might be: the program code has been written, reviewed, tested, documented and deployed.

User stories

User stories are commonly used as a de facto notation for backlog items. The technique was first introduced by Kent Beck in his book *Extreme Programming Explained: Embrace Change* (Beck, 1999), but, arguably, they were popularised by Mike Cohn in his book *User Stories Applied for Agile Software Development* (Cohn, 2004).

Often described as a **placeholder for a conversation**, a user story is a quick way of capturing the desired behaviour of a software product feature (functional requirement) at a high level, by describing something that a user needs the software product to do.

A key strength of user stories is their simple construction, being made up of the following elements:

- **User (who)**: identifies the user role[4] that needs to interact with the software to perform a particular task or achieve a particular goal.

- **Functionality (what)**: identifies the required function performed in response to the user request.

- **Value (why)**: identifies the expected value (or the business benefit) the user achieves by using the functionality.

Figure 4.9 shows an example of a user story for a meeting room booking system. This has been handwritten on a card, following the 'Three Cs' concept (card, conversation, confirmations) introduced by Ron Jeffries (Jeffries, 2001), but they can equally be captured on sticky notes, during a group collaboration session or story writing workshop.

The front of the card contains the basic story using the standard format: 'As a ... I want ... so that ...' but it also contains a name for the story (to aid discussions about the story between the various stakeholders involved in the development of the software),

---

4   A user role represents a collection of potential users who share common tasks or perform common functions.

a unique identifier (to aid backlog management) and the agreed priority and size of the story. The priority and size will be explained later.

The back of the card contains a set of statements referred to as confirmations. These provide additional clarity around the requirements for the feature to aid the prioritisation and sizing process.

When a user story is first created, it contains just the story text itself, and optionally a name and unique identifier. The confirmations typically come next, during backlog refinement sessions, and the priority and size follow later. Practice relating to user stories varies from team to team. Some teams include the prioritisation and sizing of the stories within the backlog refinement sessions, while others include the prioritisation and sizing as part of iteration planning. Additionally, some teams bypass the definition of confirmations and jump straight to the definition of acceptance criteria (not shown in Figure 4.9), which are used to make the story testable.

Figure 4.9 Example user story for a meeting room booking system

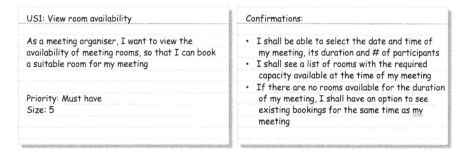

Gherkin scenarios

Defining acceptance criteria for requirements has long been regarded as a best practice approach for making software requirements testable. The criteria are defined as part of Requirements Engineering (see Chapter 5) and evaluated during user acceptance testing, after the working software has been built.

Requirements Engineering is not prescriptive in terms of the format used to express acceptance criteria, but a popular approach used by Agile development teams is to define a series of test scenarios using the Gherkin language, which is an integral part of the behaviour-driven development (BDD) approach to software engineering. BDD is explored further in Book 3 of this series, *Delivering Digital Solutions*.

Using a simple language syntax based around the structure 'GIVEN ... WHEN ... THEN ...', BAs and software developers can specify the desired behaviour of a software feature, captured as a user story, which can form the basis of tests to ensure that the feature has been correctly developed and 'behaves' according to the needs of the end-users.

An example scenario for the user story in Figure 4.9, defined using the Gherkin syntax, is shown in Figure 4.10.

Figure 4.10 Example Gherkin scenario for user story in Figure 4.9

> **Given** I am on the 'View available rooms' screen
> **When** I enter the date, time and number of
> attendees for my meeting
> **Then** I am presented with a list of rooms available
> for booking

In practice, there will be a number of separate Gherkin scenarios for the same user story, just like there would be multiple acceptance criteria for a given requirement. All criteria/scenarios must be true during acceptance testing for the feature to be deemed fit for purpose.

MoSCoW prioritisation

Prioritisation is an essential component of Agile software development. Things are constantly prioritised and reprioritised to make sure that the development team deliver the most important features of the product before concentrating on some of the less critical ones.

Agile development is particularly suited to MoSCoW prioritisation, which was developed to support iterative software development with incremental product delivery. The approach is summarised in Figure 4.11, which focuses on the prioritisation of iteration backlog items – in the form of user stories – for development within a given iteration. The technique could also be used to prioritise backlog items for inclusion within a given incremental release. This is explored further in Chapter 6.

In Figure 4.11 the MoSCoW categories (M, S, C, W) have been annotated onto the user stories (in the form of sticky notes). The relative sizes of the stories have also been annotated in circles in Figure 4.11. Relative sizing is discussed below.

The MoSCoW categories are often misunderstood, especially the distinction between 'must have' and 'should have', as they are both deemed mandatory. This means they are both essential to having a complete, robust product. However, the 'must have' features are deemed to form a **minimum viable product (MVP)**. In other words, if a 'must have' feature is not completed during the iteration, the iteration has not resulted in a viable working product, which goes against Agile principles 1, 3 and 7 (see earlier in this chapter). Consequently, the development team's primary goal for an iteration is to complete the MVP (sometimes referred to as the **minimum usable subset**).

Another challenge that often impedes the effective usefulness of MoSCoW is that the 'W' ('won't have this time') is often interpreted differently to the original concept. Some practitioners have abbreviated this category to 'won't have', which is then interpreted

Figure 4.11 Overview of the MoSCoW prioritisation technique

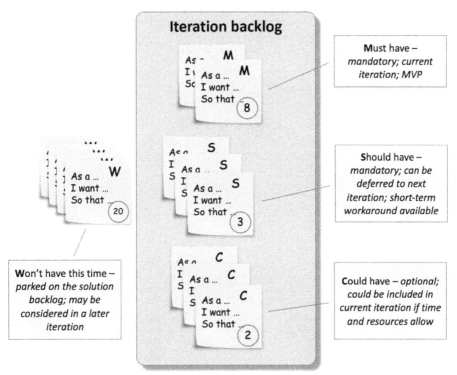

as 'won't have at all' rather than 'won't have this time'. This has led to the introduction of variants such as 'want to have but won't have this time' or 'would have'. Another confusion for some practitioners is that items categorised as 'won't have this time' during iteration planning do not actually make it into the iteration backlog, as they are essentially parked on the solution backlog for later consideration, when they may become mandatory (must have or should have) to achieving a subsequent iteration or release goal.

Planning Poker

Planning Poker is an estimation technique based on the Wideband Delphi technique, which was refined and popularised by Mike Cohn (Cohn, 2005). With this technique, user stories are assigned a size – relative to each other – based on the perceived complexity and effort required to realise the story as working software during a development iteration.

The size of a story agreed during the Planning Poker session is typically expressed as a number of **story points**, although other schemes are used such as **T-shirt sizes** (e.g. S, M, L, XL). Story points are not intended to equate to any tangible unit of time or effort, but, as long as they are allocated in a consistent manner, they can still be used as a basis for planning an iteration when combined with the concept of **velocity**, which is explored in Chapter 6.

To inject an element of fun into the process, special packs of playing cards can be used, which have a set of possible sizes printed on the cards, as shown in Figure 4.12.

Figure 4.12 Planning Poker cards

A counterargument to the practice of assigning story point estimates to backlog items (the **#NoEstimates** movement) is gaining traction within Agile software development teams. #NoEstimates challenges the necessity and value of traditional estimation practices, with advocates arguing that estimating work often wastes time and provides little value, as estimates are frequently inaccurate and do not directly contribute to delivering working software. Instead, #NoEstimates focuses on delivering small, well-defined increments of value and prioritising continuous delivery and feedback loops. By emphasising flow efficiency and reducing overhead, teams aim to make steady progress without relying on time-consuming estimation processes.

Agile boards

In order to implement the concept of transparency, which was introduced as one of the three pillars of an empirical approach earlier in this chapter, Agile development teams use a simple board that can be a physical board on the wall of an office or a virtual board provided by a software tool.

Agile boards take many shapes and forms, and Agile development teams determine the structure based on their needs and particular ways of working. Figure 4.13 shows how a simple Agile board can be used to help an Agile development team manage the day-to-day work within a development iteration.

In Figure 4.13, the sticky notes shown in the *backlog* column are user stories, but those in the other columns represent individual tasks required to realise the story as working software. The estimates on the tasks refer to effort in terms of hours of work required. These tasks and their estimates are determined during iteration planning.

Figure 4.13 Indicative layout of an Agile board

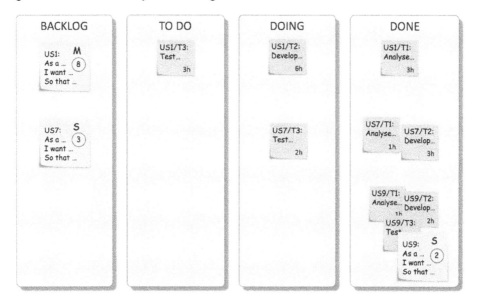

As a development iteration progresses, the team moves the sticky notes from column to column to reflect their progress. The board is typically updated during the daily stand-up meetings. When all of the tasks for a given user story are in the *done* column, and the DoD has been met, the story is deemed to be complete and is also moved from the *backlog* column to the *done* column.

Burndown charts

Agile boards are helpful to provide visibility of the development team's progress during a development iteration, but they are not so helpful in terms of identifying potential bottlenecks that may threaten the team's ability to complete the iteration goal.

Burndown charts focus the team on the work still to be done within an iteration, by plotting how many story points worth of development is remaining at the end of each day. The example in Figure 4.14 shows the position at the end of day 7 of a two-week (10 working days) iteration.

Figure 4.14 Example burndown chart

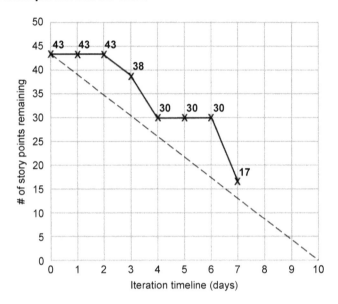

The example in Figure 4.14 shows that the planned velocity for the iteration (total number of story points in the iteration backlog) is 43 (indicated by the data point at day 0). At the end of days 1 and 2 the number of story points remaining is still 43. This shows that none of the stories is yet complete. However, at the end of day 3, the story points remaining is 38. This represents a 'burndown' of 5 story points, which shows that stories worth a total of 5 story points have been completed. This may be a single story of 5 points, two stories of 3 points and 2 points, or some other combination.

The ideal burndown (if the team were to complete the same amount of story points each day, which would never happen in practice) is plotted using a dashed line. This helps to identify where the team may be at risk of not completing the planned stories during the iteration (where the actual burndown starts to move further away from the ideal burndown). For example, the remaining story points are stuck at 30 for three days, but thankfully drops to 17 at the end of day 7, which is almost back on track.

Other techniques

Aside from the techniques just described, use cases, prototyping, storyboards and wireframes are also widely used in Agile approaches. Use cases are discussed in Chapter 7 and prototyping, storyboards and wireframes are covered in *Designing Digital Solutions*.

PART II   DEFINING THE SOLUTION

5 REQUIREMENTS ENGINEERING

INTRODUCTION

Requirements Engineering (RE) can be considered as a sub-discipline within business analysis. It comprises a set of practices that collectively enable practitioners (typically BAs) to elicit, define and manage good-quality, fit-for-purpose requirements. However, before continuing to explore RE, it is useful to clarify what is meant by a requirement. The International Institute of Business Analysis (IIBA®, 2005) define what a requirement is in their Business Analysis Body of Knowledge (BABOK):

> A usable representation of a need ... Requirements focus on understanding what kind of value could be delivered if a requirement is fulfilled.

While this chapter will introduce a range of commonly used techniques, detailed coverage of each is outside its scope. More in-depth coverage of the techniques relevant to RE, and business analysis generally, is provided in the BCS book *Business Analysis* (Paul and Cadle, 2020).

WHAT IS REQUIREMENTS ENGINEERING?

Although the origins of RE can be traced back to software engineering in the 1960s, RE as it is practised today was formalised in the seminal book *Requirements Engineering: Processes and Techniques* (Kotonya and Sommerville, 1998) and has been refined in various editions of the BCS book *Business Analysis*, now in its fourth edition (Paul and Cadle, 2020).

RE involves the following key elements, which are explored further throughout this chapter:

- a framework that practitioners can follow and replicate from project to project;
- a set of techniques that can be used at each stage within the framework;
- standards that define what is meant by 'good' requirements; and
- stakeholder roles (often referred to as the actors within RE) with specific responsibilities.

Although RE was first introduced within linear software development projects, it has since evolved to embrace iterative development, and therefore is just as valid with Agile development projects. However, the way in which the RE practices are adopted varies depending on whether a linear or iterative approach is being followed.

A FRAMEWORK FOR REQUIREMENTS ENGINEERING

The RE framework provides a structure and a mechanism to manage and control requirements work. It incorporates three key activities (elicitation, analysis and validation) underpinned by a set of best practices for managing requirements, which is achieved through appropriate documentation, as shown in Figure 5.1. The way these elements are connected in the diagram reflects iteration and feedback.

Figure 5.1 A framework for Requirements Engineering

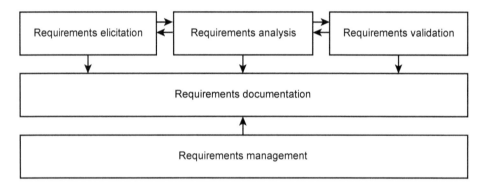

As Figure 5.1 suggests, there are three stages of the requirements process underpinned by two supporting sets of activities:

Requirements elicitation   This stage focuses on identifying the requirements. It involves understanding the needs of the customer or end-user to identify the features or functions that need to be provided by the solution (functional requirements), and the service levels and constraints that must be complied with when those features are realised (non-functional requirements). There are many techniques that can be employed at this stage, depending on the circumstances of the individual project.

Requirements analysis	Once requirements have been elicited, they are examined methodically (both individually and collectively) to see if they meet the standards of 'good' requirements. Where necessary, requirements may be elaborated and improved and sometimes split into smaller, more granular requirements ready for validation. During the analysis stage it is often necessary to undertake further elicitation work to ensure that the requirements meet these necessary quality criteria. This may also identify further possible requirements.
Requirements validation	When the analyst has reviewed and refined the requirements so that the quality criteria are met, they are reviewed again by a nominated group of business and technical stakeholders, to confirm their fitness for purpose. This validation review may focus on an individual, or limited set of, requirements to determine whether they are 'ready' to progress into development. Alternatively, this may be a more structured review of the entire set of requirements for a project or solution, including supporting documentation, leading to baselining and sign-off of the requirements before they are passed to the next stage of the solution development process, whether that is to build or procure a solution that realises the requirements.
Requirements documentation	Documentation is critical to taking a best practice approach to requirements. During elicitation the analyst keeps a record of each requirement as it is uncovered, and throughout the rest of the requirements process the documentation is elaborated, checked and refined. Textual requirements can be supplemented by graphical models (see Chapter 7) to represent the functionality of the proposed digital solution and the data needed to support that functionality.
Requirements management	Requirements management essentially places a series of governance mechanisms around the practice of RE. This ensures that changes to requirements are managed, as relevant to the context, and that the delivered solution meets the needs of the business commissioning the solution development work.

Configuration management (version control) is needed to make sure that the correct versions of the various documents are being worked on; change control is needed to make sure that 'scope creep' does not occur; and it is important to be able to trace requirements back to their source and, if relevant, forward to their resolution. |

ROLES IN REQUIREMENTS ENGINEERING

The responsibility for Requirements Engineering primarily rests with BAs. However, in order for RE work to be successful, contributions are needed from a range of stakeholders with specific responsibilities. These stakeholder roles (also referred to as actors in RE) can be categorised into two broad groups: business representatives and the project team, as shown in Figure 5.2.

Figure 5.2 Roles in Requirements Engineering

Business representatives	The project team
Project sponsor	Project manager
Product owner	Business analyst
Subject-matter expert	Solution developer
Business staff	Solution tester

Collaboration and cooperation

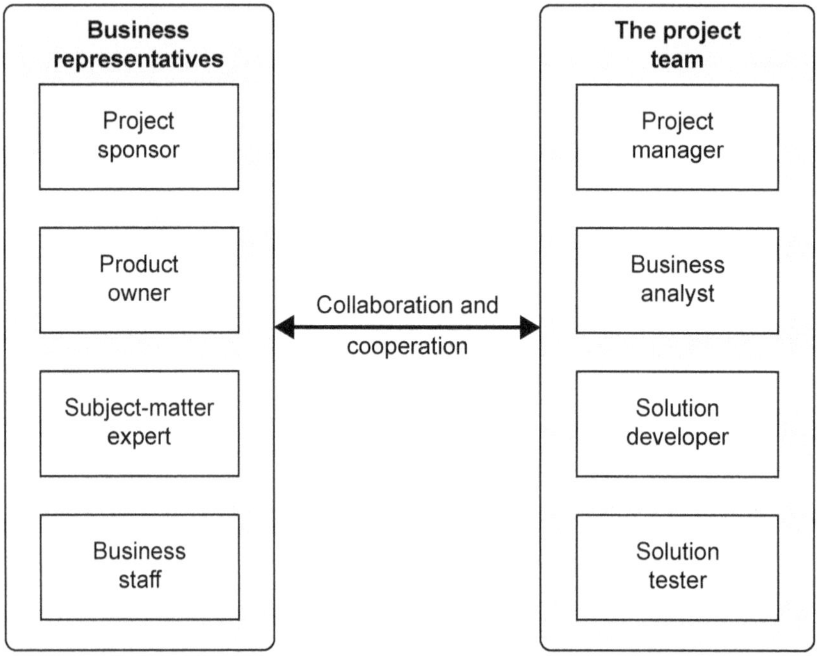

Project sponsor	This role – also known as the senior responsible owner/officer or accountable executive – is the person who 'owns' the project within the business and is (or should be) accountable to the organisation for the delivery of its business benefits.

The project sponsor has the following responsibilities:

• to agree the Project Initiation Document (PID)/terms of reference (ToR) for the RE work;

• to make funds and other resources available to the project;

• to rule on any conflicting requirements where the BA cannot negotiate agreement;

- to approve any requirements documentation as an accurate record of the business needs and, where necessary, to provide formal approval and sign-off;
- to accept the project deliverables;
- to deliver the agreed business benefits predicted in the business case; and
- to confirm that these benefits have been realised.

Product owner   This role originated from the Scrum Agile method but has since become widely adopted by organisations deploying a variety of Agile approaches. The product owner essentially owns the solution (product) backlog on behalf of the project or business sponsor[5] and is empowered to make decisions regarding the development and ongoing maintenance of the product.

The product owner has the following responsibilities:

- to determine product (solution) backlog items in alignment with business needs;
- to determine the relative priorities of backlog items in terms of which items are to be developed in a development iteration and which items are to be deployed in an incremental release;
- to make decisions on behalf of the organisation during the development and deployment of product features; and
- to resolve conflicts between requirements or priorities.

Subject-matter expert (SME)   This role (also known as domain expert) provides a broader, and often more objective, perspective than other business staff (see below). SMEs can be people within the organisation with extensive knowledge of a particular business area, or external business or management consultants specialising in a particular business domain, who can provide expertise not available within the organisation, such as industry best practice. The SME's responsibility is to provide advice regarding the requirements, especially in the following circumstances:

- where the organisation is considering adopting the latest industry best practice or innovations within the industry; and
- where the organisation wishes to introduce a new product or service that they do not yet fully understand.

---

5   The term 'business sponsor' is often used by organisations and development teams that undertake work outside a project framework, for example a team that is dedicated to the ongoing development and maintenance of a particular product throughout its life.

Business staff

These are the people who carry out the work of the organisation and who will be adopting a new process and/or digital solution, and therefore they are key sources of requirements. This role can be further broken down into two sub-roles:

- **Business managers** have a broad knowledge of how the organisation operates, and therefore can describe processes, business policies and business rules that must be addressed by the requirements. As managers of specific business areas and groups of end-users, they may have requirements of their own, such as transition requirements (e.g. the need for training and data migration during the transition from the old ways of working to the new). They can also play a pivotal role in the definition of non-functional requirements, which represent service levels that the proposed solution must meet. In addition to defining their own requirements, they may also be the owners of requirements that originate from end-users working in their business area.

- **End-users** are the people who will primarily be using the proposed solution. They may be customers of the organisation or they may be employees who are actors within one or more business processes, and need to use the proposed solution to perform their job. Either way, end-users are key stakeholders when it comes to defining functional requirements as they can provide insight into the ways that the proposed solution can support specific tasks that they need to complete, through the use of techniques such as scenario analysis and prototyping. In addition to defining requirements, end-users are also actively involved in user acceptance testing (UAT) to ensure that the developed solution meets their needs and supports their working practices.

Project manager

The project manager (PM) is accountable to the project customer (project sponsor) and has overall responsibility for achieving the project objectives and delivering the project deliverables. In the case of RE, this typically involves a digital solution.

The PM has the following responsibilities:

- ensure the project objectives are achieved in line with constraints (such as time and budget) defined in the PID or ToR;
- control the scope of the project to avoid the potential for scope creep;
- divide the project work into measurable tasks, each with defined deliverables;
- allocate tasks to project team members;

- schedule when tasks will start and finish, taking account of any dependencies;
- monitor the progress of tasks and take any remedial action necessary to avoid delays; and
- manage any risks associated with the project.

Business analyst (BA) This role is an integral part of the solution development team and is primarily responsible for defining high-quality, fit-for-purpose requirements. As detailed earlier in this chapter, this includes activities such as eliciting, analysing, specifying, validating and managing requirements. By doing so, the BA ensures that business needs are thoroughly analysed and accurately reflected in the team's chosen approach to deliver the desired solution and achieve business objectives. A critical aspect of this role is facilitating effective collaboration between business and technical stakeholders.

Solution developer Solution developers are responsible for creating the digital solution based on the requirements defined by the BA. They write program code in the chosen programming language and transform it into executable software. During the RE process, developers also assess the technical feasibility of the requirements.

In Agile development projects, where the solution evolves across multiple timeboxed development cycles (iterations), developers build and refine a series of high-fidelity, evolutionary prototypes. To facilitate this process, solution developers work closely with BAs and solution testers, ensuring a shared understanding of the requirements and the establishment of clear acceptance criteria to validate the working solution.

Solution tester The solution tester collaborates with the BA and solution developer to establish acceptance criteria that help the development team to ensure they are building the correct solution. These criteria also enable end-users to verify, through UAT, that the solution meets both their needs and the business objectives. Solution testers play a key role in the development process by creating test scripts for end-users to utilise during UAT and conducting dedicated testing. This includes specialised testing, such as performance testing and penetration testing, which are further explored in *Delivering Digital Solutions*.

In addition to the above roles, other stakeholders may also be involved in RE work. For example, a quality assurance or project office function may be responsible for checking the quality of the requirements documentation during the validation stage.

REQUIREMENTS ELICITATION

The verb 'elicit' means to draw out – for example, to draw out a response or to draw out information. In RE, **requirements elicitation** literally means to draw out requirements. This is because stakeholders do not always know, or cannot always articulate, their requirements, so the BA needs to use their skill and a set of techniques to draw them out. This involves understanding the needs of the customer and end-users to identify the features or functions that need to be provided by the solution (the functional requirements), and the service levels and constraints that are placed on the solution (the non-functional requirements).

Knowledge types

One of the difficulties in eliciting requirements relates to 'tacit' knowledge. The two most common forms of tacit knowledge are:

- information, ideas and concepts that people think are so widely known that they do not bother to mention them; and
- information, ideas and concepts that people do not know they know as they have become so second nature to them, that they are not even aware of them anymore.

Elicitation techniques

Some methods of requirements elicitation (e.g. observation and scenario analysis) are better than others for discovering tacit knowledge, but none of these techniques is fool-proof, and BAs must constantly be on the look-out for areas where tacit knowledge may exist.

Elicitation techniques may be broadly classified as qualitative or quantitative. However, these categories are not definitive and some techniques straddle the boundaries between the two types. Qualitative techniques focus on non-numerical data, such as descriptions, themes or observations. They are particularly useful for exploring concepts, ideas and meanings. Elicitation techniques that are primarily qualitative include:

- interviews;
- workshops;
- focus groups;
- observation;
- shadowing;
- scenarios analysis; and
- prototyping.

These techniques involve a degree of subjectivity on the part of the BA and the users and other stakeholders they are working with.

Quantitative elicitation techniques involve numerical data that can be measured, counted or quantified. They are particularly useful for exploring patterns, relationships and statistical analysis. Elicitation techniques that are primarily quantitative include:

- questionnaires (and surveys);
- document analysis;
- record searching;
- special-purpose records; and
- activity sampling.

These techniques provide more objective and measurable data.

Types of requirement

When defining requirements for new digital solutions or modifications to existing solutions, BAs typically focus on 'what the system is required to do'. These requirements are referred to as 'functional' requirements. However, Paul and Cadle (2020) define four major types of requirement that must be considered in an RE project. These types can also be grouped into two high-level categories: business and solution, as shown in Figure 5.3.

Figure 5.3 Types of requirement (© BCS Learning and Development Ltd)

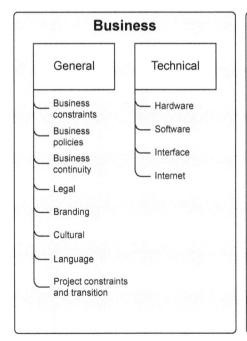
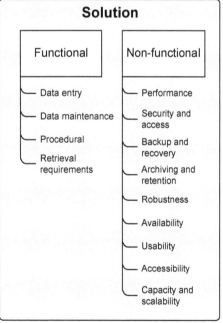

General requirements	These are high-level, overarching business requirements that define the need to comply with business policies such as branding standards and cultural and language needs. They are often broad in scope and can be decomposed into more specific functional and non-functional requirements (NFRs). Business continuity also comes under this category and can be decomposed into backup and recovery NFRs. Transition requirements (such as the need to undertake data migration and provide training in new features) and project constraints (such as time frame and budget) also fall under this requirement type.
Technical requirements	These are also overarching business requirements but they relate specifically to technical policy and constraints. These may include the need to use specific hardware and/or software platforms or programming environments. Another common example of a technical requirement is the need to interface with other solutions (often referred to as interoperability), which forms a key part of the overall technical architecture of the organisation.
Functional requirements	These define what a proposed solution is expected to do – the features it offers to users. They include system processing (identified as procedural in Figure 5.3), such as 'the solution shall identify when an invoice is overdue for payment and alert the financial controller'. They also include data entry and maintenance, and retrieval, such as displaying data on screen or generating a report or document.
Non-functional requirements (NFRs)	These define the service standards within which the solution should operate or with which it should comply – the qualities it must exhibit. For example, 'the result of a query shall be displayed within two seconds of the user pressing the enter key'. NFRs cover a broad range of issues, as shown in Figure 5.3.

There are often connections between different types of requirement. For example, a functional requirement to display a customer's account balance may be associated with NFRs concerning access rights, speed of response and usability. Similarly, a general requirement to comply with data protection legislation would typically be expanded into more detailed functional and non-functional requirements – for example, to disclose to customers the information that is held about them (functional) and to restrict access to personal data (non-functional).

The IIBA BABOK version 3.0 offers an alternative system for classifying requirements, with four main categories:

Business requirements	Like the general requirements previously described, these are high-level statements of the goals, objectives and needs of the organisation as a whole. They focus on what the business needs to achieve, not how it will be achieved.
Stakeholder requirements	These are statements of the needs and expectations of individual stakeholders, or groups of stakeholders. Stakeholders can include customers, end-users, business managers and anyone else impacted by the project's outcome. They tend to be at a higher level of abstraction than the solution requirements.
Solution requirements	These define the features and functionality to be provided by the proposed solution (typically software applications) that address the business and stakeholder requirements. They elaborate the specifics of how the solution will work. Solution requirements are sub-divided into functional and non-functional requirements, as previously described.
Transition requirements	These describe what is required to make a transition from the existing processes and systems to the proposed new ones. They might include training for users, data migration plans, or changes to existing business processes. Unlike the solution requirements, these do not describe features that are to be developed in the proposed solution, but represent temporary requirements that will not be needed again once the new solution is in operation. These are considered a subtype of general requirements in the classification system defined by Paul and Cadle, as previously described.

Whichever classification scheme is used, categorising requirements serves two key purposes:

1. It forms a basis for managing the requirements – requirements of a similar type can be grouped and considered together or assigned to different stakeholders for review, or later in the SDLC to different members of the development team.

2. It provides a useful checklist for the BA to prompt them to consider all types of requirements, rather than just focusing on the functional requirements.

REQUIREMENTS ANALYSIS

When requirements are first elicited, they often lack the detail and precision necessary to be translated by the solution development team into a working solution. Requirements analysis is concerned with ensuring that the elicited requirements have been developed clearly, in a well-organised manner and are appropriately documented. Therefore, requirements analysis can be said to turn the raw requirements into good-quality, fit-for-purpose requirements. That is that they are 'ready' to be taken forward by the development team and translated into a working solution (typically a software solution), irrespective of the approach taken to acquire or develop the solution (see Chapter 3).

Inevitably, the analysis work will reveal further questions that must be asked and so lead to more elicitation work.

Characteristics of good requirements

As the objective of requirements analysis is to ensure that the elicited requirements are good quality, there needs to be a definition of what good looks like, and therefore, the following characteristics (referred to as **requirements filters** by Paul and Cadle (2020)) are used to focus the work of the BA when analysing requirements:

Categorised	Each requirement needs to be categorised as discussed earlier.
Relevant	Requirements must be within the defined scope of the project, and should align to the project objectives, which are typically defined within a PID or ToR document, produced prior to RE work commencing.
Prioritised	The relative importance of requirements to each other needs to be established (prioritisation was introduced in Chapter 4 and is discussed further later in this chapter).
Achievable	Requirements must be technically feasible, acceptable to the organisation and affordable.
Understandable and unambiguous	Requirements must be understood consistently by the different stakeholders who are interested in them – for example, by end-users and solution developers.
Testable	Requirements must be described in a way that enables the solution to be tested to confirm that the requirement has been met.
Requirement not solution	It is easy to wrongly document solutions as requirements. The requirement must define 'what needs to be provided' rather than 'how this should be achieved'.
Consistent	Requirements must not contradict other requirements, and the formats used to define them should be consistent. This reduces ambiguity and confusion, and makes requirements validation and solution development more straightforward.
Owned	Requirements need an owner to ensure accountability, clarity and alignment throughout the SDLC. The owner of a requirement should be someone who has the authority to make decisions about the relevance and content of the requirement, and can later confirm whether the requirement has been met.

Unique   Requirements should not be duplicated or overlap with any other requirement. Often the same requirement is elicited from different stakeholders, so any duplicates need to be resolved to eliminate any unnecessary work.

Atomic   Requirements must be 'discrete' and sufficient to stand alone – not covering more than one feature. This is a key factor when prioritising the requirements and scheduling them for development. At an early stage in an Agile development project, some requirements are high level in nature or composite. These are referred to as **epics** and need to be decomposed prior to being referred for development.

Traceable   It is necessary to know the origin of a requirement so that more detail can be sought if necessary. Additionally, a record must be kept of what happened to the requirement during the design, development and testing of the solution – was it met in the delivered solution or perhaps set aside as too expensive or not technically feasible? Traceability is a key part of requirements management, which is covered later in this chapter.

Concise   Insofar as this is compatible with meeting the quality criteria already described, requirements should be described as briefly as possible as this makes them easier to understand and review.

Complete   For a requirement to be useful, it must be a complete statement of what is required and not rely on extensive reference to other documentation.

Correct   In one respect, meeting all the other criteria listed here means that a requirement is likely to be correct. However, a requirement can still be excellent in a technical sense and yet incorrect when defining what the organisation needs. This is explored in more detail under *Requirements validation* later in this chapter.

Conformant   If the organisation has a set of standards that define how requirements should be documented and phrased, these should be followed. This is also a consideration during requirements validation.

Clearly, this is a long list of quality criteria, but requirements that do not meet them are almost certain to cause problems later in the solution development life cycle.

INVEST

The acronym INVEST represents an alternative set of quality characteristics that is often used to check the quality of user stories when following an iterative (Agile) approach to solution development. The INVEST acronym was introduced by Bill Wake (2003), an XP expert, and later gained wider recognition when Mike Cohn, a prominent figure in Agile development, recommended its use in his book *User Stories Applied* (Cohn, 2004). The INVEST criteria have evolved somewhat since their introduction – for example,

Wake's original use of 'S' for 'Scalable' is now interpreted as 'Small'. However, the core principles of INVEST remain and it is a valuable tool for creating effective user stories.

User stories are checked against the INVEST criteria (see below) to determine whether they are ready to pass to the development team to be designed and built.

Independent   Each user story should not depend on others but should be discrete and atomic.

Negotiable   Each user story should provide a brief description of a required feature but be subject to further modification as a result of discussions between the system's users and developers.

Valuable   Each user story should offer an outcome of potential value to users or customers.

Estimable   Each user story should be clear enough to enable an estimate – either relative to other user stories or in terms of the absolute anticipated development effort – to be determined for it.

Small   Each user story should be small enough to be completed within a single iteration of development.

Testable   Each user story should have clearly defined measures that will enable the developed functionality to be tested, and fitness for purpose determined.

Requirements analysis activities

Requirements analysis may be seen as checking each requirement to ensure that it meets the quality characteristics outlined above. However, in practice, it involves several separate tasks:

- elaborating and refining requirements;
- checking congruence with business objectives and the business case;
- checking quality against predefined criteria;
- checking feasibility;
- structuring (organising) the requirements;
- prioritising the requirements;
- packaging the requirements for delivery; and
- dealing with overlapping, duplicate and conflicting requirements.

Requirements analysis can apply at two levels: each individual requirement and the set (or subset) of requirements. Sometimes the activity applies to each individual requirement and sometimes it applies to the complete set (or a subset).

Prioritisation of requirements

Requirements must be prioritised because there is rarely enough time, money or resources to meet all the requirements identified, and decisions need to be made about which ones to meet and which to set aside.

Various prioritisation schemes (see Chapter 6) are used within organisations, but the scheme that has become dominant in the solution development world, especially Agile software development, is MoSCoW (see Chapter 4).

With linear projects, the prioritisation of requirements is undertaken at the project level, because the requirements are baselined and signed off early in the project, and determine what will be built and delivered. With Agile projects, prioritisation can be undertaken at different stages. For example, prioritisation of the functionality that will be *delivered* in the next release, or prioritisation of the requirements that will be *developed* within a given development iteration. Therefore, it is important to consider the interpretation of the priority categories within the context of what is being prioritised.

The prioritisation of requirements often involves extensive negotiations between the BAs and the various stakeholders, who may well have differing views about what is important.

REQUIREMENTS VALIDATION

Once the elicited requirements have been analysed and refined, they should be ready for the final stage of the RE process: validation. This involves a review of the requirements by a selected group of stakeholders who are external to the project team. The aim is to confirm that the defined requirements correctly and completely state the features and characteristics to be fulfilled by the proposed solution. The requirements may be defined using different documentation and modelling techniques. For instance, a formal Business Requirements Document (BRD) may have been produced that includes a complete set of requirement descriptions and models. Alternatively, a solution backlog may act as a repository for the requirements, features and other work items to be delivered.

Validation plays a key role in both linear and iterative projects and is the responsibility of business representatives such as business staff, the project sponsor and the product owner.

Validation in a linear project

A formal review process (Figure 5.4) is followed when a linear project approach has been adopted. The complete set of documented requirements – typically contained in a BRD, as described below – are reviewed to determine if they accurately define the business requirements for the solution, and will ultimately meet the business needs and anticipated beneficial outcomes, identified in the business case that would typically have been signed off prior to the RE work commencing.

When requirements are deemed to meet the required quality standards, they are signed off and baselined, and subsequently progress into solution design and development.

After baselining, any subsequent changes proposed for the requirements are subject to change control and configuration management, discussed later in this chapter.

Figure 5.4 Formal review process

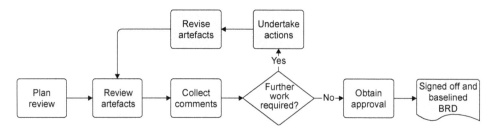

Unlike analysis, which is conducted primarily by the BA, the group responsible for validating requirements should include a range of stakeholders. Each reviewer has different responsibilities as they are obliged to examine the requirements from a particular perspective. The following roles and responsibilities should be represented within the review group:

- The **business sponsor** ensures that the requirements are all in alignment with the business objectives and do not concern areas that are outside the scope of the project.

- The **business analyst** is responsible for providing information about the requirements and may take responsibility for presenting them to the review meeting.

- **Owners** of the individual requirements, or their representatives, ensure that the requirements express the business needs clearly and correctly, without ambiguity. It is the responsibility of the business representatives to be satisfied with the requirements before accepting them.

- **Subject-matter experts** ensure that the requirements reflect correct business practice and/or industry best practice.

- The **solution architect** ensures that the requirements provide a firm basis for developing and delivering the solution within the architectural context for the organisation.

- **Developers** ensure that the requirements are technically feasible.

- **Testers** ensure that the requirements are testable.

- **Project office representatives** ensure that the requirements are compliant with business standards and policies, and that correct quality review procedures have been followed.

Validation in an iterative (Agile) project

Requirements validation in an Agile solution development project works very differently to its linear counterpart. This is a consequence of not having a complete set of good-quality requirements at the point of validation.

Girvan and Paul (2024) explain that, in an Agile project, requirements can be validated in many ways:

> In the early stages of a project, documentation may be reviewed to validate that the outline scope and the initial business requirements are well-defined and provide a basis for further elaboration.
>
> When using Agile, requirements are often validated once they have been developed so are demonstrated within a working solution. Prototypes and models may also be used within requirements validation.

Once a backlog has been established, the backlog items are subject to ongoing refinement so that any requirements allocated to an iteration are in a sufficiently defined state and are ready (that is, they meet the **definition of ready (DoR)**) for development work to commence. Girvan and Girvan (2022) define DoR as:

> A set of defined and visible value-focused criteria that must be met by a work item before work can commence.

Girvan and Paul (2024) continue to explain that:

> The DoR ensures that a development team can develop an item without this work being delayed or prohibited by external dependencies. The team must have the external information needed to start and complete the development work. This includes information about data requirements, access permissions, user interface design constraints, and dependencies on other teams.

The review and refinement of backlog items may include the development of scenarios and low-fidelity prototypes. Some requirements (epics) are considered large and/or highly complex and need detailed analysis and further decomposition prior to being considered ready for development.

In addition to reviewing backlog items, Agile requirements validation also takes the form of frequent inspections by business stakeholders of the product being built. These take place at the end of each iteration. Any changes arising are reflected in an updated solution backlog, and ultimately in the delivered working solution. Formal sign-off is not generally required in iterative/Agile projects, but some form of acceptance may be required in some organisations.

REQUIREMENTS DOCUMENTATION

This element of RE is concerned with making sure an appropriate level of documentation is produced to fully define the requirements, and support the management of the requirements.

Unfortunately, there is a lack of agreement in the IT community as to what the final document to be produced is called. The following terms are commonplace: Business Requirements Document, requirements specification, statement of requirements, user requirements specification and even functional specification. The term 'specification' tends to be more prevalent with dedicated systems analysts than BAs. The BRD is considered below as this tends to be the standard within business analysis.

The Business Requirements Document

Figure 5.5 shows the typical contents for a BRD, as defined by Paul and Cadle (2020).

Figure 5.5 Contents of a BRD (© BCS Learning and Development Ltd)

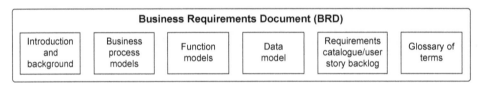

| Introduction and background | This section provides a description of the business situation and explains the background to the project in terms of the business drivers. It clarifies the scope and objectives of the work and ensures that all stakeholders are aware of the business context for the requirements and subsequent solution. |
| Business process models | Any new or enhanced software solution must support the associated business process changes. 'To-be' process models should set out the vision for the new processes and may be accompanied by more detailed tasks. 'As-is' processes that are to be revised may also be included here for additional clarity or explanation of existing problems or issues. Swimlane diagrams are commonly used to show the flow of tasks within a process and the actors who perform the tasks. 'As-is' and 'to-be' process models and swimlane diagrams are covered in the book *Business Analysis* (Paul and Cadle, 2020). |

Function models	The functionality of a required solution is often more easily understood by looking at models, so these can be provided to supplement the functional requirements. Diagrams showing the proposed functionality of a software solution may be included here, such as context diagrams and use case diagrams. These diagrams provide an excellent overview of the solution and offer a means of structuring the requirements. Use case diagrams are also supplemented with use case descriptions, which provide additional detail regarding how an end-user needs to interact with the new system when using a particular piece of functionality. Context diagrams, use case diagrams and use case descriptions are explored further in Chapter 7.
Data model	The data requirements needed to support the required solution functionality (captured in the function models) are also more easily understood using models. An understanding of the data required to be stored and manipulated within a software solution can be provided in the form of a data model. Object class models (often referred to as *class models*) or entity-relationship diagrams (ERDs) are commonly used to represent the data requirements. They also capture the business rules that underpin the storage, use and deletion of data. These data models can also be cross-referenced with function models to identify gaps and inconsistencies in the underlying requirements (see Chapter 7).
Requirements catalogue/user story backlog	Information about each individual requirement may be defined using text. This may be in the form of a requirements catalogue or a backlog of user stories. While the user story format (see Chapter 4) is suitable for functional requirements, non-functional, general and technical requirements may be better described using the requirements catalogue format. The requirements catalogue and user story backlog can also be supplemented by other techniques such as decision tables and matrices, which are useful for defining complex business rules. Further details of the requirement attributes defined in a requirements catalogue are provided below.
	The requirements catalogue concept tends to be more prevalent in linear projects where a comprehensive set of requirements is signed off and baselined prior to being passed to the solution development team. However, even where a backlog of user stories is used in an iterative project, the backlog items may be elaborated as the project progresses to arrive at a more comprehensive requirements catalogue by the end of the project, which can be helpful when supporting and maintaining the solution post-delivery.

The use of backlogs to manage requirements is explored in Chapter 6.

Glossary of terms   Providing a glossary of terms helps to remove ambiguity from requirements. Any terminology used within the document, or specific to the organisation, that may otherwise confuse or mislead readers should be explained in the glossary.

The requirements catalogue

The requirements catalogue is a repository of requirements with a separate entry for each requirement. Each entry comprises the following attributes that collectively define the requirement:

ID   A unique identifier for the requirement.

Requirement name   A short descriptive phrase (also known as the requirement title) that indicates what the requirement concerns. This enables the requirement to be found quickly in an index or summary of requirements.

Version   The current version number of the requirement for version control purposes.

Status   The current status of the requirement (e.g. draft, reviewed, signed off, baselined).

Business area/ domain   A reference to the business area(s) to which the requirement relates or whose managers need to approve the requirement.

Source   Where the requirement came from. This could be an individual or a source document such as an organisational policy statement.

Owner   The individual who will be asked to sign-off the requirement and who needs to confirm that it has been satisfactorily met by the solution.

Stakeholders   In addition to the source and the owner, people who have an interest in the requirement and who should be consulted about it.

Requirement type   See the discussion earlier in this chapter.

Description   A more detailed statement (than the requirement name) to fully describe the requirement.

Priority	A value recorded about the requirement to indicate its relative importance. The priority helps the development team to determine which requirements need to be built and delivered first. In a linear project, the entire set of requirements is prioritised as part of analysis and confirmed during validation, before the requirements are handed over to the development team. In an iterative (Agile) project, the iteration and release backlogs are prioritised during iteration and release planning sessions, respectively. While various prioritisation schemes are in everyday use, the MoSCoW system (see Chapter 4) has become widely adopted, especially in Agile development projects.
Associated non-functional requirements	If the requirement is categorised as functional, this entry is used to record any non-functional issues specific to that functionality.
Acceptance criteria	The criteria to be used during acceptance testing to determine whether the solution has satisfactorily met the requirement. The criteria take the form of a series of assertions that must be true during acceptance testing. The requirement's acceptance criteria are *not* the same thing as, or even an alternative to, an acceptance test specification, but should indicate the principles on which acceptance will be based.
Rationale/ justification	A statement encapsulating the business justification for the requirement. This information is useful when prioritising the requirements and may be cross-referenced to specific benefits in the business case.
Related documents	Cross-references to documents where further information can be obtained about the requirement. For example, a reference to (among others):

- the notes summarising an interview;
- the business case;
- the PID;
- the business process models produced during the discovery stage of the business change project; and
- the use case and class diagrams produced to model the requirements.

Requirements modelling is covered in Chapter 7.

Related requirements	Cross-references, represented by requirement IDs, that identify other requirements that should be considered in conjunction with the requirement to which the entry relates. These references may indicate dependencies between multiple requirements and are particularly useful when performing impact analysis for proposed changes.
Resolution	The outcome of the requirement. There are several possible outcomes: implemented, deferred for future consideration, merged with another requirement or dropped.
	The resolution is used to record the decision and the timing of this decision, and is needed to ensure the traceability of the requirement (see below).
	Additional entries may also be used to provide more extensive traceability, such as a detailed description of everything that happened to the requirement as it progressed through the solution development life cycle. This could include cross-references to the design documentation and key events such as when the requirement was tested and released, and the release version number.

REQUIREMENTS MANAGEMENT

Requirements management comprises a set of practices used to ensure the successful delivery of the requirements and the management of any changes that occur throughout the solution development project. Three main aspects of requirements management need to be considered: configuration management (including version control), change control and traceability.

Configuration management and version control

Identifying the latest version of a requirement, understanding its relationship with other requirements and documentation, and determining its current status are critical objectives of requirements management, which are achieved through configuration management (CM). CM systematically organises and manages configuration items (CIs), which, in the context of RE, are the individual requirements.

Beyond organising requirements, CM also handles the dependencies between them, which is crucial for assessing the impact of proposed changes. By maintaining links and interdependencies, CM enables teams to efficiently manage multiple iterations, including tracking revisions, comparing changes and restoring previous versions, when necessary, which ensures that stakeholders have access to accurate and up-to-date information at all times.

When combined with version control, CM strengthens traceability, prevents conflicting updates and provides a transparent audit trail of changes. Together, these practices ensure that requirements are managed systematically and effectively, supporting business goals and aligning with stakeholder expectations.

Change control

In the context of RE, change control is a structured process for managing modifications to requirements throughout the SDLC. It ensures that any proposed changes are thoroughly evaluated for their impact on the project scope, timeline, cost and other requirements, before approval or rejection.

Change control involves documenting the change request, analysing its implications, obtaining stakeholder consensus and updating relevant artefacts such as requirements documents, traceability matrices and test cases. Implementing a clear and consistent change control process can prevent scope creep, maintain alignment with project objectives and ensure that the final product continues to meet stakeholder needs and expectations while minimising disruption and facilitating the successful integration of changes into the development process.

Traceability

The ability to trace a requirement back to its origin (source) enables the BA to identify who to consult to clarify any information about the requirement, and who needs to authorise any changes to the requirement (owner). Similarly, the ability to trace a requirement forward to its realisation as a feature in the delivered solution is essential so that, once the solution goes live, those maintaining it can understand why certain features have been implemented as they have, before they make any changes or updates. This is known as horizontal traceability and is demonstrated in Figure 5.6.

Figure 5.6 Horizontal traceability

FORWARDS TO

Source/origin
of requirement

Requirement/
backlog item

Digital solution

BACKWARDS FROM

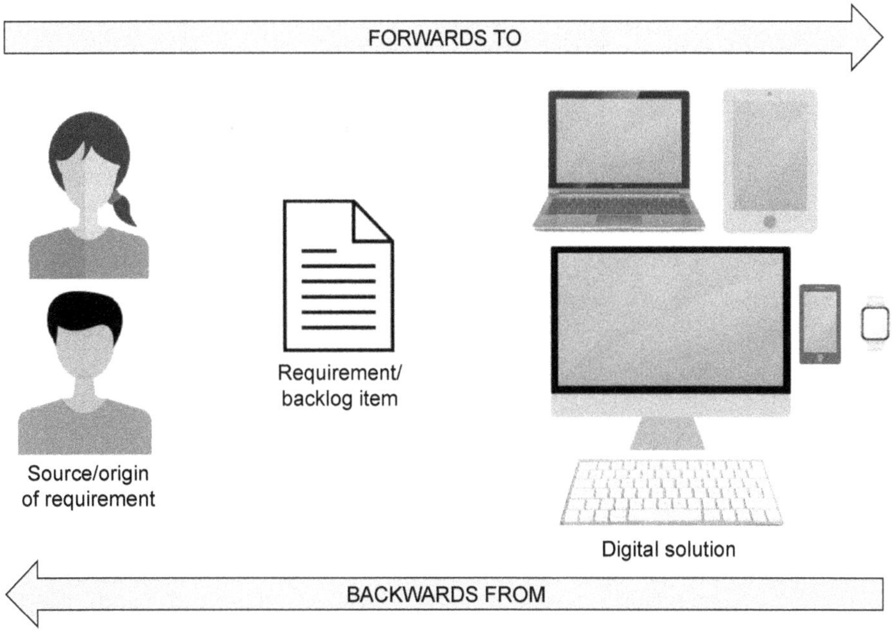

A further form of traceability (vertical traceability) provides the ability to trace a solution level requirement up the hierarchy of requirements to the business-level requirement(s) from which it was derived, and beyond to a more strategic business objective (objectives and key results (OKRs)) or critical success factor (CSF). Similarly, to trace from a business objective to the business requirements and further down to the solution requirements that address the objective/CSF, as shown in Figure 5.7.

Figure 5.7 Vertical traceability

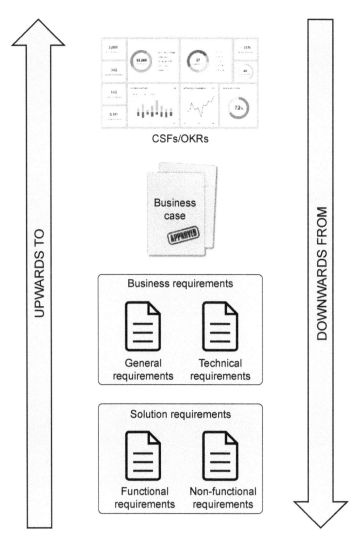

A prerequisite for successful change control, configuration management and traceability is the ability to uniquely identify and cross-reference requirements and record the source and owner of each requirement (see *Requirements documentation* earlier in this section). This can be difficult to achieve without using a requirements management or computer-aided requirements engineering (CARE) software tool. CARE tools are covered in more detail in Chapter 8.

REQUIREMENTS ENGINEERING AND OFF-THE-SHELF SOLUTIONS

Some organisations adopt a 'buy first' policy, whereby they will only consider building a bespoke solution if a suitable off-the-shelf solution is not available. Where an off-the-shelf solution is being sought, good-quality requirements are still essential and RE is still relevant. However, pursuing an off-the-shelf solution introduces some additional types of requirements (discussed below). Procuring an off-the-shelf solution also necessitates some changes to the requirements process because the requirements, as well as being categorised and prioritised, are also weighted to support the selection process.

All the elements of the RE framework are still required, but BAs must take special care to ensure the requirements define *what* the users want the solution to do and do not unduly constrain *how* it is to work. Inevitably, when a ready-made solution is procured, some compromise is required between what the stakeholders would ideally like and what can practically be delivered within the limitations of the available solutions. If the end-users insist on the solution working in a particular way, customisation of the off-the-shelf product may be required, leading to the MOTS approach (see Chapter 3).

While most digital solution development projects carefully capture and define the functional and non-functional requirements for the solution, with an off-the-shelf solution there are some additional types of requirement that are also critical, which are discussed below.

Product requirements

Product requirements are concerned with the way the product has been designed (product design requirements) and built (technical and conformance requirements). These can be important when considering the product's ability to be integrated as part of a wider solution with other solution components, such as bespoke applications and applications developed by other suppliers.

A list of typical product requirements is provided in Table 5.1.

Table 5.1 Typical product requirements

Product design requirements	Technical and conformance requirements
• Software architecture approach adopted • Design principles adopted • Configurability	• Hardware platform and resources • Software development language used • Database platform used • Use of open standards (e.g. communication protocols and data formats) • API and communication protocols • Cloud-based (SaaS) solution or on-premises (on-prem) – desktop versus browser-based • Operating systems supported • Browser technologies supported

Supplier requirements

When procuring an off-the-shelf solution, it is essential to consider specific requirements related to the supplier or vendor. For instance, the supplier may need to demonstrate qualities such as good corporate citizenship, financial stability and market maturity (supplier stability requirements). Additionally, a critical factor to evaluate is the supplier's overall responsiveness and engagement throughout the evaluation and selection process. These elements should be identified as explicit requirements so that they can be weighted in terms of their relative importance and compared to other types of requirements.

A list of typical supplier requirements is provided in Table 5.2.

Table 5.2 Typical supplier requirements

Supplier stability requirements	Supplier citizenship requirements	Supplier responsiveness requirements

• Size and location
• Financial stability
• Marketplace knowledge
• Ownership and structure
• Accreditation
	• Promotion/ encouragement of equal opportunities
	• Diversity and inclusion policy
	• Health and safety policy
	• Anti-bribery policy
		• Impressions and recommendations from reference sites
		• Approach to:
		  ▪ performance measurement
		  ▪ issue management and escalation

(Continued)

Table 5.2 (Continued)

• Quality assurance procedures	• Charity and donations policy	▪ arrangements for 'trial use'
• Use of automated tools	• Trade union policy	▪ continuous improvement
• Insurance		▪ innovation
• Dispute-handling procedures		▪ responding to change
• Outstanding legal or commercial issues		▪ collaborative working
		▪ taking and acting on customer feedback
		▪ ensuring adequate resources are available/in place

The evaluation of supplier requirements can be complicated by reseller networks where the supplier is not necessarily the developer of the product.

Operability requirements

Digital solution development projects often overlook the broader ecosystem in which the software product will be implemented, operated and supported. Key decisions, such as opting for a cloud-hosted solution or adopting a subscription-based model (such as pay-as-you-go or monthly payments), are frequently made during the project initiation phase and should be defined as requirements to guide the selection and procurement process. Operability requirements may also outline the mechanisms for obtaining vendor support and maintenance, including specified service levels for responses to and resolution of support issues. Additionally, it is essential to consider contingency plans for scenarios where the supplier may go out of business and become unable to provide continued support and maintenance.

Initial implementation requirements

Similarly to operability requirements, specific requirements for the initial implementation of the new solution are also often overlooked, or at least not formally defined. Commonly referred to as **transition requirements**, these include installation and configuration of the product itself, data migration and/or creation, the training of users and the changeover strategy from old working practices to new ones.

Imperatives

Imperatives are requirements that the solution must definitely provide for it to be considered in the selection process. If an imperative is not met, then the product is excluded from the selection process. Imperatives can be found in any category of requirement.

Weighting requirements

Before the evaluation and selection stages of an off-the-shelf solution procurement process can begin, the requirements are weighted. Weighting of requirements is similar to prioritisation during bespoke development projects, as it provides a basis for considering the relative importance of requirements. However, unlike the prioritisation schemes that are used with bespoke developments, weighting uses numeric values. This is essential to enable later scoring of candidate products.

Weightings can be applied at category level (as per the example in Table 5.3) and individual requirement level.

Table 5.3 Requirements weightings (by category)

Category	Weighting (relative importance)
Solution requirements	
Functional	30
Non-functional	10
Product requirements	
Product design	2
Technical and conformance	8
Supplier requirements	
Stability	12
Citizenship	3
Responsiveness	4
Implementation requirements	
Initial implementation (deployment)	6
Operability	5
Other constraints	
Cost constraints	18
Time constraints	2
TOTAL	**100**

Supplier responsiveness is not shown in Table 5.3 because, while important, this is not something that can be directly assessed within the evaluation process. Supplier responsiveness is typically determined later in the selection process.

Cost constraints are not strictly a category of requirements, but their inclusion during the weighting of requirements provides an opportunity to weigh cost against other considerations during the evaluation and selection process. For example, cost may be more critical than supplier citizenship for some customers. Similarly with time, when comparing different product offerings, it may be more important to select a product that can be implemented more quickly over a supplier that offers a less costly solution.

Weightings are only considered for products and suppliers that meet all the imperatives. If a product or supplier does not meet an imperative, the product is typically excluded before applying the weightings.

In addition to weightings for each category, individual requirements within each category are also weighted, but this time a 0–5 scoring system is used, as per Table 5.4 (adapted from Tate, 2015).

Table 5.4 Individual requirement scoring system (after Tate, 2015)

Score	Classification	Description
5	Mandatory	Imperative. Solutions without explicit support for even one 5-weighted requirement will be excluded from the selection process.
4	Critical factor	Critical to the success of the solution, but not so important that they single-handedly disqualify a candidate.
3	Major factor	Solutions should consistently score well against this type of requirement to be credible.
2	Minor factor	Some significance. A bonus if supported.
1	Trivial	Of little importance and therefore only slight influence when selecting solutions.
0	Not significant	Support for this requirement should not influence the choice of solution at all.

6 MANAGING REQUIREMENTS WITH BACKLOGS

INTRODUCTION

The concept of a backlog was introduced in Chapter 4. Backlogs are a key feature of Agile development approaches, as they provide a means of prioritising and controlling the features that will be developed and delivered as a digital solution development project proceeds. However, they are equally useful in more linear, traditional approaches where a digital solution is to be delivered in stages. In fact, the backlog concept can even be employed in projects that do not involve digital technology at all – for example, an office reorganisation.

In digital solution development, multiple backlogs are used to manage the work of a development team and ensure the requirements for the solution are appropriately managed.

This chapter primarily focuses on how backlogs are managed in product-based Agile methods such as Scrum and XP, but a backlog can also be used in other circumstances. For example, Kanban applies continual throughput of development with no concept of an iteration. Instead, the next most important requirement/task is worked on next and the backlog is continually reprioritised.

THE SOLUTION BACKLOG

The solution backlog is the master backlog for a digital solution development project. The concept was first introduced by Ken Schwaber and Jeff Sutherland in 1995 as part of the Agile development method Scrum, where it was referred to as the **product backlog**. The Scrum Guide (Schwaber and Sutherland, 2020) describes the product backlog as:

> an emergent, ordered list of what is needed to improve the product. It is the single source of work undertaken by the Scrum Team.

While Scrum is most commonly associated with software development, it is not limited to software, hence the use of the more general term 'product', which is defined in the Scrum Guide as:

a vehicle to deliver value [which] has a clear boundary, known stakeholders, well-defined users or customers ... a product could be a service, a physical product, or something more abstract.

In practice, the product backlog comprises a list of features (functional requirements) to be incorporated within the product under development, but it can also contain other types of requirement, such as non-functional requirements (NFRs – performance, usability, availability and so on), and technical requirements (such as the technology or standards to be used during the development of the product), and even general requirements, such as high-level business policies that constrain the development. Additionally, the backlog can also contain defects found during testing or operational use, and proposed enhancements to an existing solution.

Backlog items

When introducing the product backlog concept, Scrum was not prescriptive regarding the format of backlog items. However, since its introduction within the XP Agile development method (one year after the introduction of Scrum), the **user story** (see Chapter 4) has emerged as a de facto standard for defining a backlog item. This is because it captures the essence of a requirement at a high level without getting bogged down in details. Some items remain at this level throughout the development project and may eventually be de-scoped altogether. However, most items will be refined (backlog refinement), so that they are at an appropriate level of detail to enable the development team to build the feature into the product during a particular development iteration.

Sometimes a backlog item is just too big to be developed into working functionality within a single iteration. Such items (referred to as epics, maintaining the analogy with stories) require splitting (or slicing) into multiple items, each decomposed item being small enough to be developed during a single iteration.

Backlog items are prioritised by the product owner after consultation with the business stakeholders, and with support from BAs. The priority assigned to a particular backlog item depends on its business justification, value, risk, required delivery date, estimated complexities and interdependencies with other requirements. Prioritisation is considered further below.

THE RELEASE AND ITERATION BACKLOGS

Most Agile projects use multiple backlogs to organise and manage requirements. Scrum defines two: the product backlog (solution backlog) and the Sprint backlog (**iteration backlog**). The Scrum Guide defines the Sprint backlog as:

the set of product backlog items selected for the Sprint ... a plan by and for the Developers ... a highly visible, real-time picture of the work that the Developers plan to accomplish during the Sprint in order to achieve the Sprint Goal ... [it] is updated throughout the Sprint as more is learned [and] should have enough detail that they can inspect their progress in the Daily Scrum.

Although Scrum supports the incremental delivery of the product during its development, it does not explicitly define the concept of a **release backlog**. Instead, it takes a release-when-ready approach. However, many Agile development teams use a third release backlog to help manage and control each incremental release. The relationship between the three backlogs is shown in Figure 6.1.

Figure 6.1 clearly shows that the release backlog is a subset of the solution backlog, and that the iteration backlog is a subset of the release backlog.

The release backlog is populated during release planning, an event where the project team, along with the product owner, prioritise the remaining solution backlog items (those that have not yet been actioned) to create a separate backlog comprising just the items from the solution backlog that the product owner deems necessary for the next release of the product. The items in the release backlog will typically require multiple iterations of development to build before the product can be released. Consequently, a third backlog (the iteration backlog) is required to manage the subset of items from the release backlog that are being worked on by the team in the current iteration.

Figure 6.1 uses shading to indicate that some of the items in the solution and release backlogs will have been refined and deemed 'ready' to be developed into working software (the dark items), while some will require further refinement (the lighter items). Some, if not all, of these lighter-shaded items will be epics that will be split into multiple smaller items during backlog refinement.

Figure 6.1 also clearly shows that all items in the iteration backlog are fully refined and 'ready' for development.

THE PRODUCT BACKLOG ICEBERG

An alternative way of visualising the solution backlog and how it relates to releases and iterations is the Product Backlog Iceberg, which was popularised by Mike Cohn, a well-known figure in the Agile community and the author of several books on Agile practices.

Using the analogy of an iceberg, Cohn demonstrated that the visible portion of the product backlog (above the water) comprises the items (user stories, features or tasks) that are currently prioritised and included in either the current Sprint or the current release. These include the highest priority (at the moment) items and those expected to be addressed in the near-term. Below those are the items that are not currently prioritised but do form part of the long-term vision for the product. They can include planned future enhancements, 'technical debt' (things that may be done to improve the

Figure 6.1 Relationship between different backlogs

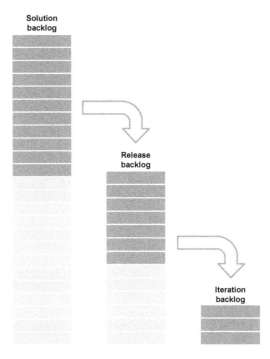

quality of the code, for example) and things that may result from market research or customer demand in the future. Figure 6.2 illustrates the concept.

Figure 6.2 **The Product Backlog Iceberg** (after Cohn, 2004)

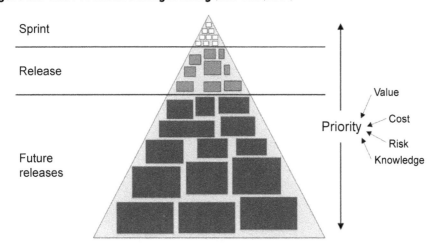

The value placed on a particular item depends on a consideration of its value to the organisation, the cost of implementing it, any risks involved and the state of knowledge about it. Clearly, all of these are liable to alteration as time passes and circumstances change.

In Figure 6.2, the larger blocks of functionality represent the epics (described earlier). By the time each item has been assigned to an iteration, it will need to be defined with more granularity, usually as smaller user stories.

USER STORY MAPS

An alternative approach to organising features across the various levels of backlog is by creating user story maps. Developed by Jeff Patton (Patton, 2014), these provide a visual way of arranging and understanding user stories and how they fit together to meet user needs, which can help teams with planning the development of a product to be deployed over a number of incremental releases, as shown in the example in Figure 6.3.

The top two rows are often referred to as the story backbone and comprise high-level activities and the tasks required to complete them. The activities are sometimes referred to as themes, and the tasks are essentially epics (big stories). The more granular stories are identified below their associated epic, and should ideally be small enough to develop within a single iteration. These stories can then be grouped for delivery in a particular release, represented by the horizontal bands.

As each story is completed, a tick can be added to provide a visual confirmation. Other symbols can also be used to show stories currently being worked on or where further development is blocked. The latter is determined as an impediment during a daily stand-up meeting, and the team leader (Scrum Master) takes responsibility for resolving the blockage to enable development to continue.

REFINING THE BACKLOG

Unlike the requirements catalogue in a linear development project, which tends to be fixed at the start and then only altered though a formal change control process, a backlog is constantly refined as an Agile project progresses. This is through necessity due to the iterative nature of Agile development projects, and is actually a strength of the Agile approach, which, in contrast to linear approaches, embraces change as the project progresses.

Changes occur during digital solution development projects for a variety of reasons including:

- Business requirements are clarified though discussion with different business stakeholders.
- Advances in technology enable features that were not originally possible.
- Business stakeholders change their minds about what is needed.

Figure 6.3 User story map showing stories assigned to releases (after Patton, 2014)

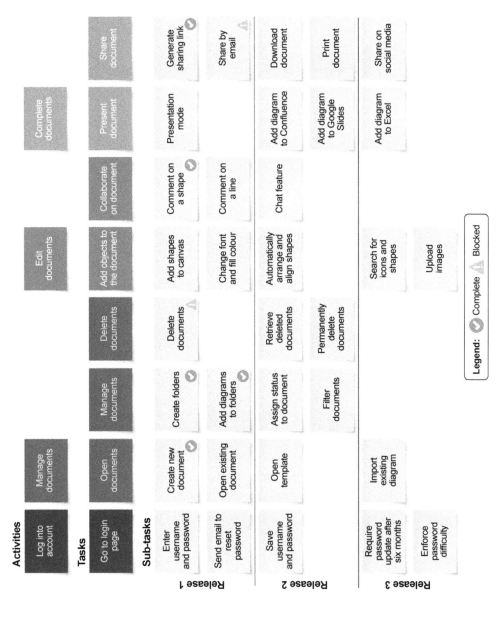

111

Depending on the situation, backlog refinement could involve any or all of the following:

- splitting one backlog item into two or more smaller items to enable each to be completed in a single development iteration;
- adding new items to meet new user requirements that have come to light;
- combining low-level items into larger groupings, especially when these are to be considered in detail during later iterations;
- changing the relative priorities of the backlog items to reflect changing business or user priorities; and
- adding more detail (such as acceptance criteria or Gherkin scenarios) to the highest priority items, especially those that are to be included in the next planned iteration.

The Product Backlog Iceberg (Figure 6.2) reflects this changing refinement as the items towards the top of the iceberg are smaller and more precisely defined than those towards the bottom.

While Agile methods such as Scrum are not prescriptive about how backlog refinement is undertaken, a common approach used is a Three Amigos session. These sessions involve a conversation between the BA, the developer (or representative of a team of developers) and the tester (or representative of a team of testers) where each party ensures they correctly understand the story under review and collectively agree a set of acceptance criteria, which forms the basis for design, development and testing.

PRIORITISING BACKLOGS

In an Agile development project, backlogs are continually prioritised and reprioritised. This provides clarity for all concerned about what is important at a particular point in time, and what can be put to one side (at least for the time being), ensuring that the work of the team is always focused on the immediate business priority rather than what was important at the beginning of the project, or during the last release.

Facilitating early prioritisation enables the project team to spend time on those things that matter the most, so that early benefit can be achieved and trust developed between technical and business stakeholders.

As mentioned earlier, prioritisation of the backlog is the responsibility of the product owner, in consultation with business and technical stakeholders, and is often assisted by BAs. Defining a goal for the iteration or release can help the team to focus on those things that are essential to achieving the goal, those things that add value but are not essential to the goal and those things that do not contribute to achieving the goal.

There are various frameworks that can assist with prioritisation; the most popular in common use are described below.

Stack ranking

The simplest method of prioritising a backlog is to order the items in terms of their importance and urgency (when they are required), with the most important and urgent feature at the top of the stack and others being ranked after it, accordingly. When the team start to develop an item, they simply take the next one from the top of the backlog.

MoSCoW

The MoSCoW prioritisation scheme (introduced in Chapter 4) was popularised in the 1990s by Dynamic Systems Development Method (DSDM), and continues to be the de facto standard approach for many development teams that adopt iterative development with incremental delivery.

MoSCoW comprises four categories – must have, should have, could have and won't have this time – and the rules that govern these provide a basis for decisions to be made about what the project team will work on during an iteration, within a given release or over the whole project. However, as a consequence of the dynamic nature of iterative development, and the likelihood that priorities will change as the project progresses, it is not particularly useful to attempt a project-level prioritisation exercise. But MoSCoW can certainly be used to prioritise the release and iteration backlogs.

Prioritising an iteration backlog using MoSCoW
When deciding which items from the solution backlog to take into the iteration backlog, it is necessary to consider what will happen if all the items cannot be completed within the fixed timebox associated with the iteration.

By keeping the size of each item in the iteration backlog small (sizing of backlog items is considered later in this chapter), there is a better chance that items can be completed within the fixed timebox, but, due to the exploratory nature of Agile development, there is always uncertainty, so the product owner, working with the project team, must decide which items absolutely must be completed (the 'must haves') and which could be deferred if the team runs out of time (the 'could haves'). The 'must haves' are considered mandatory and non-negotiable, and the 'could haves' optional – that is, they can be completed if time allows.

The 'should haves' (like the 'must haves') are also considered to be mandatory, which means they represent important features that cannot be omitted from the product. However, unlike the 'must haves', they can be left out of the product increment being developed during the iteration, typically because there is a workaround if the feature is not available for a short time. However, unlike the 'could haves', which can be omitted from the product altogether, the 'should haves' will need to be developed at some point, and often during the next iteration, where they will potentially be reprioritised as 'must haves'.

Solution backlog items that are deemed 'won't have this time' are effectively out of scope of the current iteration goal and are not included in the iteration backlog. They can be considered to be 'parked' in the solution backlog as far as the iteration is concerned.

When using MoSCoW to prioritise an iteration backlog, project teams typically consider the 'must have' items to represent the minimum viable product (MVP). This is because, if any of the 'must haves' are not completed during the iteration, then the product increment delivered at the end of the iteration is missing features that are deemed to be essential for the product to be viable. To avoid the risk of delivering a non-viable product, the team use a 'rule of thumb' (heuristic) that states that the iteration backlog should contain no more than 60 per cent 'must haves'. The 60 per cent refers to the total number of story points estimated, not the total number of stories (backlog items). The remaining 40 per cent is typically split between 'should haves' and 'could haves'. Story points are explained later in this chapter.

A common problem experienced when using the MoSCoW prioritisation scheme is that the majority of requirements are deemed to be 'must haves'. If this were true, the flexibility derived from MoSCoW prioritisation would be removed as there are no lower-priority requirements that can be de-scoped from the current iteration or release. This may indeed be indicative of the fact that the project is not suited to iterative development with incremental delivery, but is perhaps better suited to a linear approach. However, the assertion that all requirements are 'must haves' is often symptomatic of insufficient decomposition of the higher-level requirements.

Prioritising a release backlog using MoSCoW

Where a project team uses three backlogs, as demonstrated in Figure 6.1, release planning takes place before iteration planning, and therefore the release backlog (containing the features to be delivered and deployed in the next release) is prioritised before the first iteration of development for the release is planned. The same principles described above for prioritising the iteration backlog apply to the prioritisation of the release backlog. However, the release priority for a given backlog item can be different to the iteration priority for that item. For example, a feature to enable the user of a room booking application to view historical bookings may be prioritised as a 'could have' in the release backlog but a 'won't have this time' in the iteration backlog for the first iteration. The same feature could then be reprioritised to a 'could have' in the iteration backlog for the second iteration.

Kano

The Kano model (Figure 6.4) was developed by Professor Noriaki Kano (Kano et al., 1984). The model relates to product development and customer satisfaction and can either be used on its own or to complement MoSCoW prioritisation.

Kano helps to prioritise product features by considering both the objective functionality to be delivered by each feature and also the emotional impact on the customer of having that feature or not. It thus takes users' expectations and customer satisfaction into account in deciding on the prioritisation of the items in the backlog.

From the perspective of a purchaser of a product or service, Kano considers product features as satisfying three levels of need:

1. **Basic features**: These are the essential features of the product that are associated with its basic functionality. As Figure 6.4 shows, the omission of basic features from a product leads to significant customer dissatisfaction, but the inclusion of basic features does not lead to increased levels of customer satisfaction. This is because customers expect these features to be available in the product.

Figure 6.4 Kano model for prioritising product features (after Kano et al., 1984)

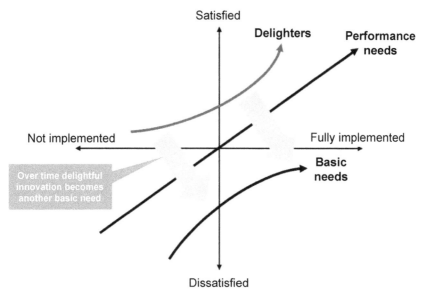

2. **Performance features**: These features will lead to increased customer satisfaction when included in the product, but if omitted will lead to some dissatisfaction.

3. **Delighters**: These are the features that are often unforeseen by the customer, but their inclusion in the product yields the most customer satisfaction. Their omission does not result in any dissatisfaction as the customer is unaware of the features until they are discovered through use of the product.

In terms of the relationship with MoSCoW, the basic features roughly translate into 'must haves', the performance features into 'should haves' and the delighters into 'could haves', although this is not an absolute mapping, and the project team needs to consider each feature on its merits and decide when they need to implement the feature.

Weighted shortest job first

Weighted shortest job first (WSJF) is commonly used in Agile and Lean methodologies, particularly within the adoption of Scaled Agile Framework® (SAFe). WSJF helps teams to prioritise backlog items by considering multiple factors, such as the relative cost of delaying implementation of the feature and the amount of work needed to implement it.

Each item can be scored using the formula:

$$\text{WSJF} = \frac{\text{Cost of delay}}{\text{Job size}}$$

Cost of delay represents the potential business impact or value lost if the work item is delayed, taking into account aspects such as lost revenue, missed opportunities, increased costs or decreased customer satisfaction. More formally, this considers the following:

- **Time criticality**: The urgency or time sensitivity of implementing the item (feature), which reflects how much value will be gained or lost based on when the item is completed.
- **Risk reduction/opportunity enablement**: This considers the potential risk mitigation or opportunity enablement that a particular feature provides, reflecting the potential impact on reducing uncertainty, opening new opportunities, or addressing critical issues.

Job size represents the effort required to implement the feature, which can be measured in various units, including story points, function points or estimated time.

By calculating WSJF for each backlog item and comparing the results, teams can prioritise their work to focus on delivering the highest value with the lowest risk and cost of delay. This helps to optimise resource allocation and maximise the potential value delivered by the team.

USE OF STORY POINTS AND VELOCITY TO DETERMINE THE CONTENT OF BACKLOGS

Determining exactly which requirements (features/backlog items/stories) to include within the release and iteration backlogs, is a key part of backlog management. This chapter has already considered the role of prioritisation in determining this, but the relative priority of the backlog items is only part of the picture. It is also necessary to consider the amount of work that would be required to implement a particular item, and associated with this, the rate at which development work is expected to proceed. This means that the size of a user story (typically measured in **story points**) and the development rate of the team (**velocity**) are also important factors when determining the content of backlogs.

Story points

Story points were introduced in Chapter 4, which described a technique called Planning Poker that is commonly used to 'size' stories. While, in principle, any numerical ranking scheme could be used, project teams typically use a variant of the Fibonacci sequence: 0, ½, 1, 2, 3, 5, 8, 13, 20, 40, 100. The story point values do not relate to any absolutes, such as the number of estimated work hours, but, in principle, the more story points a user story is assigned, the greater the work that will be involved when implementing it. Consequently, story point values are relative, which means the team 'size' stories relative to one another, commonly using predetermined 'baseline stories' to aid comparison. For example, if a story is deemed to be smaller than a baseline story of 8 points but larger than a baseline story of 3 points, then the story should be assigned a story point value of 5.

Velocity

Velocity is a metric that quantifies the amount of work a team completes during a specific time frame, typically a development iteration. It is commonly measured in story points. By analysing velocity, teams can forecast future workloads, enhance iteration planning and set realistic project timelines.

Girvan and Paul (2024) define the following approach to calculating velocity:

- Establish an estimation approach, usually by agreeing a 'standard' work item and assigning it a number of estimation units [such as story points] ... This serves as the team's reference work item, which provides a basis for estimating other items.

- Conduct development work for at least one iteration and calculate the number of estimation units completed in that iteration. This is the **baseline velocity**.

- Plan the next iteration based on being able to deliver the same number of estimation units and work at the same velocity.

- Update the baseline velocity following each iteration, using the velocity of the previous iteration to determine a rolling average. As the work progresses, and assuming everything remains constant, the team's estimation and the velocity calculation should become more accurate.

In the example in Figure 6.5, the team's velocity (also referred to as **actual velocity**) at the end of the iteration in question is 31.

Figure 6.5 Calculation of the velocity of a team

Baseline velocity at the end of the iteration = 8 + 5 + 5 + 3 + 8 + 2 = 31

Assuming that Figure 6.5 shows the iteration backlog at the end of iteration 1, when planning iteration 2 the team would use the baseline velocity of 31. If they also apply the heuristic introduced earlier (no more than 60 per cent 'must haves'), then they should not allocate more than 18 story points to 'must have' items, with the remaining 13 story points being spread equally between 'should haves' and 'could haves'.

If there are more than 18 story points allocated to the 'must haves', then the team should look again to see if any of the 'must haves' could be decomposed into smaller stories. When decomposing a 'must have' story, it is often found that not all of the decomposed stories are indeed MVP for the iteration. So, having decomposed a backlog item, the new decomposed items should be sized and prioritised until the team are happy with the mix of 'must haves', 'should haves' and 'could haves' in the iteration backlog.

If the calculated velocity for iteration 2 is 35, then the new baseline velocity would be 33. When more than three iterations have been completed, it is common to use a rolling average calculated from the last three iterations, as shown in Figure 6.6.

Figure 6.6 Calculation of baseline velocity using a rolling average

Actual velocity for iteration n = **35**
Actual velocity for iteration $n-1$ = **33**
Actual velocity for iteration $n-2$ = **37**
New **baseline velocity** = (35 + 33 + 37) / 3 = **35**

Planning a release

As well as being key concepts for planning an iteration and deciding the content of the iteration backlog, story points and velocity can also be used during release planning to determine the content of the release backlog. However, when planning a release, there is an additional consideration, which is when the team will be ready to make the release. By calculating the number of iterations of development that will be needed to build all the features required for the release, the team can determine a scheduled delivery date for the release, as demonstrated in Figure 6.7.

Figure 6.7 Calculation of the number of iterations required to deliver a release

Baseline velocity = **35**
Number of weeks per iteration = **2**
Total number of story points in the release backlog = **125**
Number of iterations required to develop release backlog items = **125 / 35 = 4** (3.57)
Number of weeks development until release is ready = **4 x 2 = 8**

If this date is not acceptable to the product owner, then the goal of the release could be revisited to reduce the scope of what will be delivered, or, as described above, the remaining release backlog items could be further decomposed, and the decomposed items reprioritised and resized until an acceptable compromise can be achieved. When revising the scope of a release, the product owner and team need to consider the impact of the missing features on the end-users and customer, and whether suitable workarounds are in place.

7 MODELLING THE REQUIRED SOLUTION

INTRODUCTION

The use of models to represent things is a practice that dates back to ancient civilisations including Mesopotamia and Egypt, where models of complex structures such as buildings or temples were produced prior to construction. In modern civilisations this would be considered a form of prototype. Prototypes are a particular kind of model, but not all models are prototypes.

This chapter discusses the use of models in digital solution development and presents a range of models from the Unified Modeling Language (UML), which, according to its original authors (Rumbaugh et al., 2005), is

> a general-purpose visual modeling language that is used to specify, visualize, construct and document the artifacts of a software system.

For many digital solution development teams, UML is the go-to standard for modelling software systems, although other useful approaches can be found in *Business Analysis Techniques: 123 Essential Tools for Success* (Cadle and Paul, 2021).

WHAT IS A MODEL?

A model is a representation of something: an idea or concept, a physical object, a situation or, in the context of this book, a digital solution. The subject of the model may already exist or may be something that is being developed but does not yet exist. A model of something that already exists is often referred to as an 'as-is' model, and a model of something that does not yet exist, but is planned for the future, is referred to as a 'to-be' model.

RATIONALE FOR MODELLING

George Box, a renowned 20th-century industrial statistician, wrote (Box and Draper, 1987):

> all models are wrong; the practical question is, how wrong do they have to be to not be useful?

This is the key to the use of models – their creation is not an end in itself but rather they are used to clarify, explore or illustrate how something (e.g. a digital solution) could or should work.

The value of modelling

Producing models takes time and effort and therefore incurs cost in a project, which needs to be offset by the value that modelling offers. There are two types of value that can be derived from the use of modelling:

Value from the act of modelling itself	A popular aphorism in Agile software development circles is 'fail fast' (often associated with the Lean Startup methodology popularised by Eric Ries (2011)). This is due to the amount of re-work necessary to correct a defect, which increases the later in development the defect is found. This principle is substantiated by studies by Barry Boehm (1981) and others.
	The act of modelling can identify defects early in the development process, and fixing them is much quicker and cheaper than performing remedial work on the working solution. Defects include incorrect model elements (derived from misunderstandings and incorrect assumptions) and missing model elements (often a result of gaps in the knowledge of the modeller or requirements gaps). The structure of models and their visual, diagrammatic representations makes these missing elements more obvious to identify and easier to rectify than a list of narrative statements.
	Additionally, as the modeller develops a model, questions often come to light that need to be answered to complete the model. This provides an opportunity to seek further clarification from key stakeholders, to remove any ambiguity in understanding.
Value of the model(s) produced	Another popular adage (of indeterminate origin), 'a picture is worth a thousand words', is often used to explain how a single diagram, with the appropriate syntax and content, can explain something more accurately and succinctly than a large amount of descriptive text – the formality of a structured model and the benefit of a standardised visual syntax being less prone to ambiguity. This is why the results of modelling – the models themselves – provide valuable documentation to aid the definition and communication of ideas.

The use of models brings significant benefits, including:

- **Improved communication and understanding between stakeholders**: For instance, the business and technical stakeholders involved in creating digital solutions.

- **Experimentation**: Ideas can be tried out and refined before expensive resources are committed to building a product or solution.

- **Validation and feasibility checking**: Key stakeholders can review models to ensure the proposed solution defined by the models is what is needed and can be delivered.

- **Gap analysis**: BAs and other business change professionals can explore the gaps between what is done now (defined in 'as-is' models) and what will be done differently in the future (defined in 'to-be' models) to ensure that requirements for change are precisely defined.

KEY MODELLING CONCEPTS

Abstraction, levelling and scope

Modelling is the act of producing appropriate models through the use of abstraction. Abstraction is the thought process wherein ideas are distanced from objects. This involves the following:

Generalising from specifics	This works by taking specific examples of something and identifying the general rules or principles that apply to them. For example, considering a smartphone, a smart watch, a tablet computer, a laptop computer and a desktop computer might lead to the general concept of a 'smart device'.
Focusing on relevant details	When dealing with a complex system, abstraction enables the modeller to concentrate on the details that matter for their specific purpose. For example, when using a map the user might focus on the roads and landmarks relevant to their trip, ignoring details like the colour of buildings.
Hiding complexity	Abstraction is often used to simplify a complex object, idea or situation, with the purpose of aiding understanding of the subject or simplifying the use of a physical object. For example, a coffee machine has a complex internal mechanism, but the user interacts with a straightforward interface (buttons and dials) that hides those unnecessary complexities.

In digital solution development, different models tend to focus on specific facets of the solution, for example its functionality or implementation. A single model is therefore an incomplete abstraction of the real thing, limited by the scope of its coverage and its level of detail, but a combination of models collectively provides a more complete description, provided they are consistent with each other.

Opaqueness of model elements

Digital solutions are often composed of multiple applications or components at various levels of granularity. Sometimes when modelling solutions it is necessary to show how the solution is decomposed into its component parts. At other times the model can focus on just the composite of the parts, particularly when visualising how it is assembled with other composite elements to deliver a larger solution.

Black box elements

The term 'black box' is used in a number of disciplines to refer to a view of an element (e.g. an entire solution or a single component) in a model where the modeller and the target audience are not concerned about the inner workings of the element, or where these are not known at the time the model is produced. A black box view focuses on the element as a whole and its links to, and dependencies on, other elements.

A **context diagram** is an example of a black box view of a whole system.[6] Figure 7.1 shows a context diagram for a sales order processing system.

Figure 7.1 Sales Order Processing system: context diagram

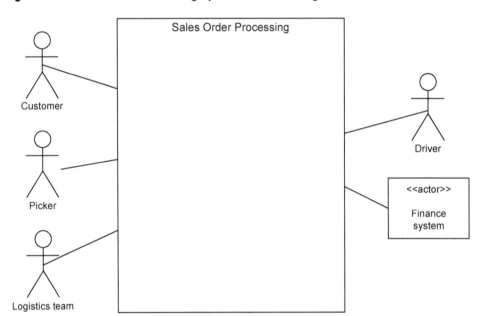

In this context diagram, the system is a sales order processing software system (application) represented by a boundary (the box) within which there are no details. The diagram does show, however, that this application will need to interact with various external entities (**actors**), including users such as customers and staff (a warehouse operative (or picker), a driver and a member of the logistics team) together with other systems (a finance system). The nature and detail of these interactions is not defined.

---

6   The context diagram in UML standardises on the use of the term 'system', but in this chapter it can be a composite of components or a single component. In this book, a system is considered to be a digital solution.

This model is referred to as a **conceptual model** as it provides a high-level business perspective of the required solution without providing any specifics of how the solution needs to work. Context diagrams are created early on in a digital solution development project, before the solution requirements have been defined.

White box elements

The term 'white box', in contrast to 'black box', is used to refer to a view of an element in a model where the modeller focuses on the internal workings of the element. The analogy behind the terms 'black box' and 'white box' is that the viewer can see inside a white box but cannot see inside a black box. This is, of course, flawed logic as a white box is as opaque as a black box. The terms opaque and transparent would be more meaningful, but white box and black box are the de facto terms used.

A **use case diagram** (see Figure 7.2, which shows a use case diagram for the **Sales Order Processing** system) may be considered a white box view of a system, as it literally shows what is inside the box. However, strictly speaking, it still does not reveal anything about the inner workings of the system, but rather it presents an external black box view of the features it needs to provide. An activity diagram (explored later in this chapter) provides a less contentious example of a white box view of a system.

Figure 7.2 Sales Order Processing system: use case diagram

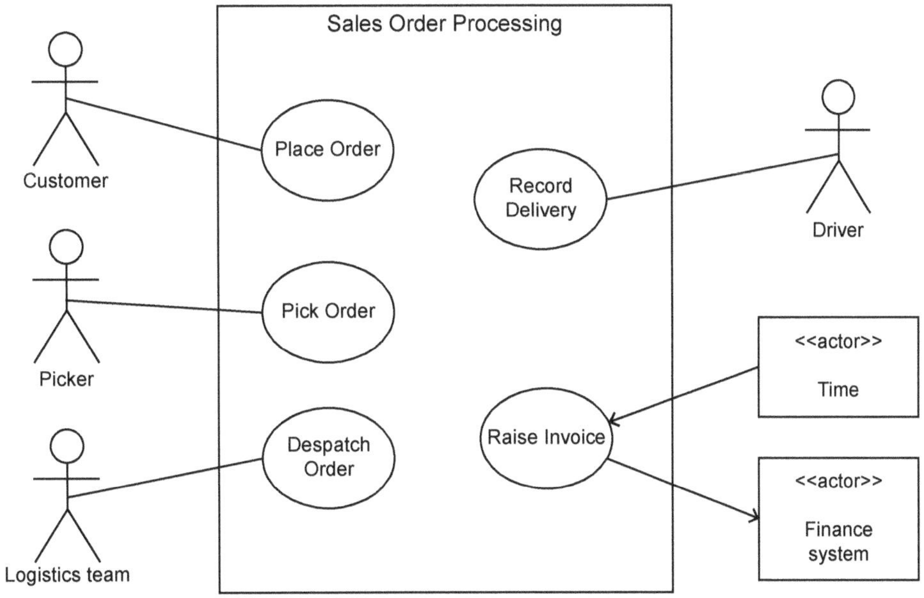

The use case diagram in Figure 7.2 would have been developed following the elicitation of initial requirements for the **Sales Order Processing** system. It highlights key functional areas needed in the solution, represented by the use cases (depicted as ovals or ellipses and labelled with verb + noun phrases), which correspond to the functional

123

requirements. The diagram also illustrates the actors who will interact with each piece of functionality in the form of associations, shown as lines connecting the actors to the relevant use cases.

Note the addition of the **Time** actor, which wasn't present in the context diagram. This would suggest that, while eliciting the requirements, the author of the diagram (typically a BA) discovered that the new solution needed to automatically raise invoices, and that this feature would be triggered at a point in time – hence the inclusion of time as an actor rather than showing the use case associated with an end-user (user role) such as a sales ledger clerk. The use of time as an actor is also a contentious issue for UML purists, but can be helpful to clarify early on the need for an automated process.

The **Raise Invoice** use case is of particular interest because it is associated with two separate actors: **Time** and **Finance System**. Additionally, the associations are **unidirectional** (denoted by the arrow heads pointing in only one direction). This indicates that one of the actors (**Time**) initiates the interaction with the system (denoted by the arrow pointing from the actor to the use case) and the other (**Finance System**) receives output from the order processing system (denoted by the arrow pointing from the use case to the actor).

When creating use case models, the concepts of **primary actor** and **secondary actor** may also be important. Although not explicitly defined in UML, it is commonly accepted that the primary actor is the one that gains benefit/value from the use case and the secondary actor is necessary to complete the task. In the example in Figure 7.2, the **Finance System** may be considered the primary actor and **Time** the secondary actor.

LEVELS OF MODEL AND MODEL ELEMENTS

As is evident in Figures 7.1 and 7.2, models can be built at varying degrees of detail or granularity. One common approach is to classify models as either business level or solution level (referred to in UML as 'system'). In terms of the context diagram and use case diagram introduced earlier, the modeller can produce both business-level context diagrams and use case diagrams and system-level context and use case diagrams. The UML doesn't officially recognise business-level models because it was introduced as a modelling language for software systems. However, the BA community has adopted some of the UML techniques to model business systems as well as software (IT) systems.

Functional decomposition

The models shown in Figures 7.1 and 7.2 focus on an entire solution. However, digital solutions can be decomposed into lower levels of detail and, at each level, a set of functional units (processes or tasks) can be identified. There is a point at which decomposing the functionality in one form of diagram becomes less useful and a different form of diagram is more appropriate.

Goal levels

Another popular approach is to consider different goal levels that are being achieved. The actors within a business system have different goals, such as to perform a particular task as part of a business process. In terms of a digital solution, these goals should not be to use part of a system, but should refer to the outcome they want to achieve by using that part of the system. This is evident in Figure 7.2, where the use cases have been named in terms of the outcomes the feature they represent will achieve on behalf of the actor – for example, to be able to place an order or raise an invoice.

Alistair Cockburn popularised goal levels in his book *Writing Effective Use Cases* (Cockburn, 2001), in which he describes the following goal levels:

Summary goal (kite level)	Typically equivalent to an end-to-end business process goal, which will take place over an extended period (typically hours, weeks or even months) and involve a number of people and systems to perform distinct activities, each of which can be described at the user goal level.
User goal (sea level)	Equivalent to a task performed by a single person or application, in one place at one time (seconds or minutes). This goal represents a complete, meaningful objective to be achieved by the user. The mnemonic OPOPOT (one person, one place, one time) is often used to identify tasks at the user goal level.
Sub-goal (fish level)	Not a meaningful goal in its own right, but enables the achievement of one or more user goals.

Cockburn also introduced two further goal levels: **cloud level** (very high summary – not useful from a solution development perspective but can be used to identify a strategic, project or programme-level goal) and **clam level** (which Cockburn deemed to be too low). Use cases at sea level and above typically focus on requirements (the 'what?') whereas sub-goal use cases begin to describe the design of the solution ('how' the solution will realise the requirements).

MODELLING IN DIGITAL SOLUTION DEVELOPMENT

Stephen Mellor – one of the original signatories on the Agile Manifesto in 2001 – describes three very different uses of models in the context of software development (Mellor and Balcer, 2022):

Model as a sketch	The idea of a model being used as a **sketch** is that the modeller can derive value from producing informal models that don't stick rigidly to the modelling language syntax. Sketching a quick model for personal use can help the modeller to understand the complexities of a subject by omitting unnecessary details. However, this kind of model should be used with caution, especially if it is to be shared among different stakeholders.

Model as a blueprint

The concept of a **blueprint** dates back to the early 1840s, when Sir John Herschel, a British scientist and astronomer, invented a photographic printing process called cyanotype,[7] which was particularly well suited to producing a white-on-blue copy of technical drawings. Hence, the term 'blueprint' was born. While no longer used for this purpose, the term 'blueprint' is still used in modern-day parlance, relating to a technical model. Mellor's use of the term refers to a model produced to formally communicate how something should work – a specification. Such models form the basis of a kind of contract between designers and developers, but a use case diagram produced by a BA could also be referred to as a blueprint, which formally communicates a specification of requirements between BAs and designers.

Model as an executable

This refers to a discipline in software engineering called Model-Driven Architecture (MDA), where models are automatically transformed by specialist tools into executable software. MDA is explored further in *Designing Digital Solutions*.

Models are used throughout the solution development life cycle, as follows:

Definition of the required solution

Models are used during RE as blueprints for requirements; to help define *what* functionality the solution needs to provide (UML use case diagram) and *what* data is required to support that functionality (UML class diagram). Dynamic system behaviour can also be modelled to define how the solution needs to react to certain business events (UML state machine diagram).

Although not part of the UML, storyboards and wireframes are also kinds of models and these can be used to explore how an end-user might interact with the proposed solution to achieve the goal of a use case, to assist with the definition of usability and accessibility requirements. Storyboards and wireframes are considered in *Designing Digital Solutions*.

Design of the solution

During solution design, models are used as blueprints to specify a series of 'black box' software components that will be built (UML component diagram), and how those components will interact with each other to realise specific functional requirements (UML interaction diagrams). 'White box' models are also used to show how each component will be 'engineered' internally (UML class diagram and UML interaction diagrams). Wireframes (low- to medium-fidelity prototypes) can also be used to model the user interface design.

---

7   More information about cyanotypes can be found at www.graphicsatlas.org/identification/?process_id=319

Development of the solution

As introduced above, MDA is a software engineering discipline that focuses on the use of models to drive the automated development of working software using specialist tools to generate code directly from a set of models, without the need for a human software engineer. When changes are needed to an operational solution, the modeller makes changes to the underlying models and regenerates the code, rather than directly modifying the generated code. This way the models and the code are always synchronised. No-code solutions, introduced in Chapter 3, adopt similar principles to MDA but do not (typically) use the same transformation from platform-independent to platform-specific models.

Evolutionary prototypes (discussed in *Delivering Digital Solutions*) are also extensively used during the development of the solution, especially if an Agile approach is being adopted.

While the above uses of models focus on **forward engineering** (the process of defining high-level models and refining them into functional software through systematic development and implementation), **reverse engineering** of models is also a common practice. This involves analysing an existing system, application or codebase to extract higher-level models or representations, such as UML diagrams or architecture diagrams. This process is often used to understand, document or improve legacy systems, facilitate integration with new solutions or ensure alignment with updated business needs.

The rest of this chapter focuses on a range of UML models that can be used to **define** a solution. Book 2 in this series, *Designing Digital Solutions*, introduces a range of models that can be used to **design** the solution.

THE THREE-VIEW APPROACH TO MODELLING SYSTEMS

A popular approach to defining digital solutions is to use three different, but complementary, representative views as highlighted in Figure 7.3.

- **Functional**: The functional view focuses on what the solution does or is required to do – the functions or features that a system is to provide. This often incorporates the 'who?' – the people or systems that need to interact with the solution to perform this behaviour.

- **Data**: The data view considers the information that will need to be stored in the solution to support the processing defined in the functional view. It provides a structural view of data, and is therefore qualified by the term **static.**

- **Event (dynamic)**: The event view focuses on the real-world events to which the solution will need to respond. This view is also referred to as the dynamic view because it is essentially exploring system behaviour over time.

Figure 7.3 The three-view approach to modelling systems (© Assist Knowledge Development Ltd)

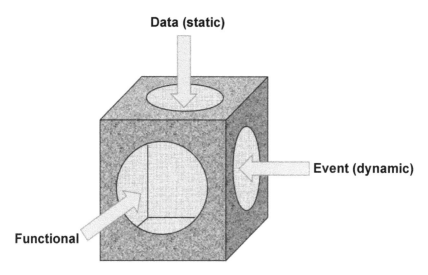

Data (static)

Event (dynamic)

Functional

Figure 7.3 visualises the rationale behind the approach: in order to gain a complete picture of a system (the box in Figure 7.3), it is necessary to look from each of three separate perspectives (equivalent to looking through the portals in the box). When applied to software systems, the analogy refers to gaining a complete picture of a system by looking at it from a functional, data and event perspective. Historically, BAs and developers considered a system from two of the three perspectives (functionality and data). This often resulted in an inconsistent set of models representing an incomplete, or incorrect, understanding of the full requirements of the system, leading to defects that needed to be corrected at significant cost with patches and workarounds after implementation.

MODELLING FUNCTIONALITY

In UML, the main tool for defining system functionality is the use case model, comprising one or more use case diagrams (e.g. Figure 7.2) supported by a set of use case descriptions (see below).

Use case diagrams

As explained earlier, each of the ovals within a use case diagram represents a **use case** – a piece of functionality provided by the digital solution. The main box represents the **system boundary** and the stick figures and smaller boxes represent **actors**, which interact with the system but are external to it. Actors can represent user roles, other systems or time. UML purists reject the idea of time as a true actor because it is merely a trigger and does not have an interaction across the system boundary. However, BAs often show time as a trigger for automated functionality that is initiated at a point in time rather than in response to a direct request from a user or other system.

Actors are connected to use cases via **associations**. Denoted by lines with or without directional arrow heads, associations represent interactions that take place between actors and the system that result in the achievement of some goal or outcome on behalf of the actor. These associations also help stakeholders to understand access requirements for the proposed system. Where the actor represents another system, the association identifies an interoperability requirement.

The use case diagram provides a useful visual representation of the functional scope of a system or subsystem, but it does not contain any detail as to how the actors actually interact with the system, or how the functionality is realised.

Use case descriptions

While there is value in the use case diagram, the real value of the use case model is in the detailed use case descriptions that accompany it, as these help to define the required functionality to a point where a software developer can design and build working functionality. The use case descriptions also provide a basis for developing test cases to validate that the developed solution performs as required.

Use case descriptions can be created in text, as UML activity diagrams or, ultimately, as UML interaction diagrams (use case realisations). A popular text-based approach to defining use cases was introduced by Alistair Cockburn (2001). Figure 7.4 shows a user goal-level description for the use case **Place Order** in Figure 7.2, written using a Cockburn-style narrative.

The ▱ symbol in Figure 7.4 indicates that this use case is a 'white box' definition, which describes what the system is doing internally as well as the externally observable behaviour – how the actor interacts with the system. A 'black box' use case description would only describe the latter. The ⨺ symbol denotes that this is a 'user goal' (sea level) use case.

The key elements of the description are:

Use case   The name of the interaction being described, which should correspond to the use case shown on the use case diagram, and the goal that is achieved on behalf of the primary actor.

Primary actor   The name of the actor that gains benefit/value from the use case – the actor associated with the use case on the use case diagram. Most use cases are only associated with a single actor, which corresponds to the user role (or sometimes another system) that initiates the interaction (functionality) and is the main beneficiary of the outcome from using that functionality.

Figure 7.4 'Place Order' use case description

Use case: Place Order ⬭ ⌁

Primary Actor: Customer (Cust)

Secondary Actor: Sales Ledger System (SLS)

Scope: Sales Order Processing System (SOPS)

Level: User goal, white box

Stakeholders and Interests:

    Picker - to generate work instructions for picking orders

    Sales ledger clerk - needs up-to-date sales figures for monitoring sales targets

Preconditions: Actor has previously created an account

Trigger: Customer wishes to make a purchase

Success Guarantees: Order details saved in SOPS; transaction added to SLS; order confirmation sent to customer

Main Success Scenario:

1. Cust initiates Place Order function
2. SOPS displays product catalogue
3. Cust selects product to order until no more products required
4. SOPS calculates order total and requests confirmation to proceed
5. Cust opts to proceed
6. SOPS requests delivery details
7. Cust selects delivery address from list of saved addresses
8. SOPS takes payment
9. SOPS sends order confirmation to cust
10. SOPS creates SLS transaction
11. Use case ends

Extensions:

5a. Cust abandons or does not respond (time-out)
    5a1. SOPS displays order abandonment message and terminates use case

7a. Required address not in list of saved addresses
    7a1. SOPS prompts for post code
    7a2. Cust enters post code and selects from list of valid addresses for that post code
    7a3. Resume from step 8

9a. Payment fails (within three attempts):
    9a1. SOPS presents payment fail options
    9a2. Cust chooses to retry payment
    9a3. Resume from step 8

9b. Payment fails on third attempt:
    9b1. SOPS displays payment failure message and terminates use case

9c. Cust abandons or does not respond (time-out)
    9c1. SOPS displays order abandonment message and terminates use case

Secondary actor	Any additional actors that are involved in the interaction and are necessary to achieve the goal, including recipients of outputs.
Scope	The name of the system (corresponding to the text that annotates the system boundary on the use case diagram) that this use case defines part of the functionality of.
Level	The level at which the use case is being defined. It is a combination of opaqueness (i.e. black box or white box) and goal level (kite – summary goal; sea – user goal; fish – sub-goal). In the case of Figure 7.4, this is a user goal (denoted by the ⤣ symbol), white box (denoted by the ▱ symbol) definition.
Stakeholders and interests	Someone or something with a vested interest in this specific system behaviour, but who does not interact with it directly. Sometimes referred to as a 'tertiary actor'.
Preconditions	Conditions that must be true for the use case to begin.
Trigger	The business event that causes the primary actor to initiate the interaction.
Success guarantees/ post-conditions	One or more conditions that must be true after the use case has successfully completed. This would typically include what data has changed in the system as a consequence of the successful execution of the functionality, but in the case of Figure 7.4 it also describes an output that has been generated and sent to one of the actors.
Main success scenario/main scenario	A step-by-step description of how the interaction between the actor(s) and the system plays out in order to successfully achieve the desired outcome (goal) of the use case, ignoring variations that may occur under certain conditions. Cockburn proposes structuring the statements using the following format: *subject + verb + object [+ prepositional phrase]*. The square brackets indicate that the prepositional phrase is optional.
Extensions	As the name suggests, these extend the main success scenario by exploring variations that can occur under certain conditions. This includes two further types of scenario: • **Alternate flows**: These describe scenarios where the interaction (or part of it) progresses differently to the main success scenario. The alternative flow is triggered by a condition that is also included in the extension entry, and the alternative steps still achieve the goal of the use case. Alternate flows are also effectively alternative success scenarios. In Figure 7.4, extension 7a is an alternative flow.

• **Exception flows**: These are similar to alternate flows but result in the actor not succeeding in their goal. Exception flows often result in an early termination of the use case that may lead to the system state remaining in its original condition, or may be some alternative outcome such as a cash machine that retains the user's card in the event that the card has expired. In Figure 7.4, extension 9b is an exception flow.

The condition is shown first followed by the steps that are taken when the condition is true. Cockburn uses the number corresponding to the step within the main scenario with a letter for each extension to identify the condition. The steps arising as a result of the condition are numbered preceded with the condition identifier. For example, in Figure 7.4, 9a, 9b and 9c denote three separate conditions that are alternatives to step 9 in the main scenario, and 9a1, 9a2 and 9a3 denote the steps that are taken when condition 9a is true.

Note that steps 8 and 10 in the main scenario contain underscored text. This indicates that the step is defined further in a separate use case description, often a sub-goal use case that is included in multiple user goal use cases. This concept is also useful for identifying reusable functionality, which may already exist as services provided by existing components. For example, **Take Payment** is likely to be a standard function or service accessed by a variety of different digital solutions. Figure 7.5 shows an amended version of the use case diagram in Figure 7.2, showing the **Take Payment** use case being 'included' as part of the **Place Order** use case.

Figure 7.5 Use case diagram showing the 'Take Payment' use case

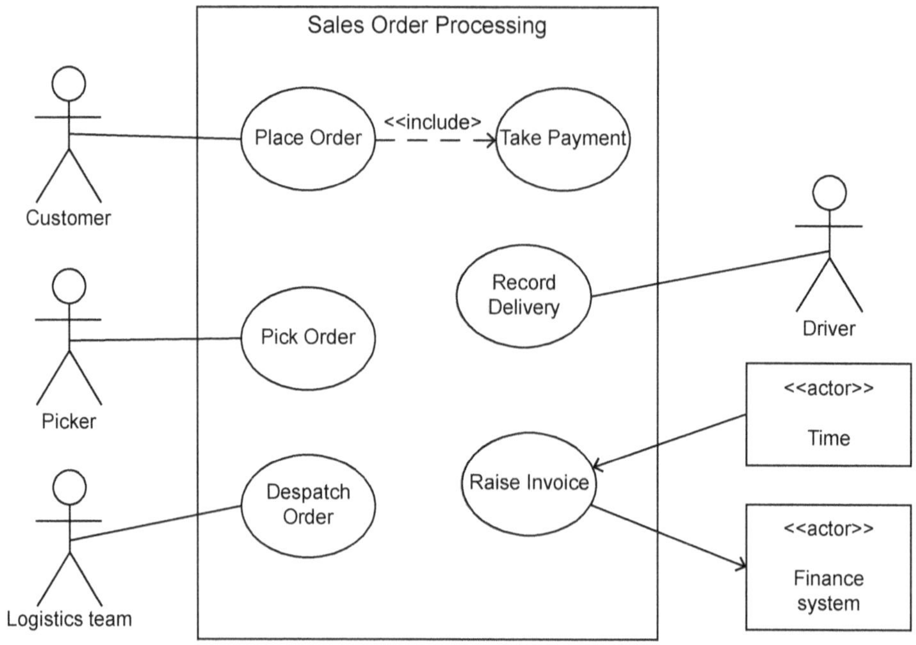

As an alternative to using a textual description of the main success scenario and extensions, as explained above, the modeller can create a more visual definition using a UML activity diagram. Figure 7.6 shows an activity diagram that represents the main success scenario and the extensions described in Figure 7.4.

The activity diagram is the UML flowchart as it shows the flow of a process (either business or system). It is relatively intuitive as the soft-cornered boxes represent the activities or tasks being performed – in the case of Figure 7.6, the steps within the use case – and the arrows show the chronological flow from one step to another. Note the use of the ⊓ symbol to denote that the activities **SOPS takes payment** and **SOP creates SLS transaction** are defined as separate activity diagrams (not shown). This is the activity diagram equivalent of the underscored text in Figure 7.4. The start of the process or activity is denoted by the ● symbol and the end by the ◉ symbol. There are four potential end points to this process, three that do not achieve the goal of the use case (annotated as *failed*) and one that does (annotated as *success*). These end points have also been attached to notes (shown as boxes with the top-right corner folded over), to explicitly show the post-conditions at each end point. The post-conditions shown against the *success* end point equate to the success guarantees in the use case description in Figure 7.4. Finally, the diamond symbols have two purposes: first, to represent decision points in the process; and second, to merge two or more paths in the process. The former is denoted by a single arrow entering the diamond and two or more arrows exiting the diamond, and the latter is denoted by two or more arrows entering the diamond and one arrow exiting the diamond. In the case of decisions, the relevant conditions are shown next to each exit path from the diamond; the path is only followed when the corresponding condition is true. For example, in the case of the first decision, the process loops back to select another product when the condition **[more products to order]** is true.

Use case scenarios and scenario roleplaying

Scenarios provide a framework for discovering the exceptions that require alternative paths to be followed when carrying out a task. They necessitate a business stakeholder (typically an end-user or SME) identifying each step required to carry out the task, and the transitions between the steps, so that the modeller can define the process using an activity diagram or use case description. This provides an opportunity to analyse what else might happen or be true, and this analysis often uncovers additional information and ensures there are no taken-for-granted elements (as a consequence of tacit knowledge, for instance). This significantly reduces the possibility of overlooking situations that could cause a solution to fail in the future.

In addition to assisting with the definition of system **usage scenarios** within a use case description, a stakeholder may also enact the scenarios, possibly using a working prototype. This is referred to as **scenario roleplaying** and can be particularly useful for validating and refining the functional and usability requirements of the solution.

The refined usage scenarios can be used by solution designers to specify *how* the proposed solution will realise the required functionality, and then, during software engineering, the solution developer can build the working prototypes to enable the users to enact the scenarios to validate that the solution works according to their needs, and to explore how everyday activities can be performed using the solution.

Figure 7.6 'Place Order' activity diagram showing interaction scenarios

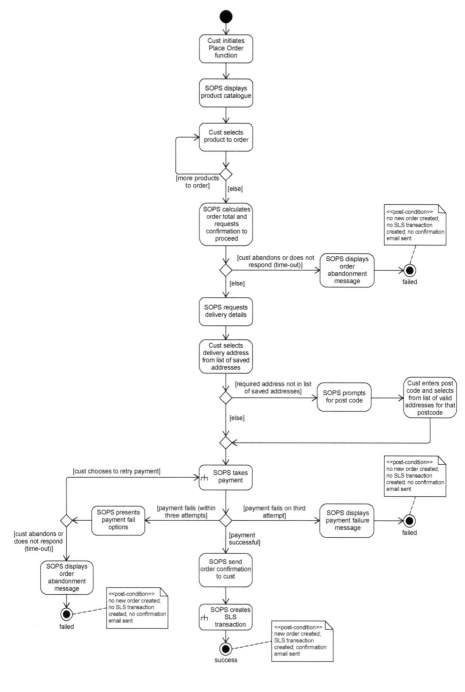

Use case scenarios can also be useful as test scenarios that again can be enacted (during UAT) to confirm that the developed solution has satisfactorily met the business and user requirements, or to support the evaluation of a COTS solution. In the latter case, the vendor can be approached to enact the usage scenarios during a demonstration of how their product can meet the needs of the business.

MODELLING DATA

In UML the main tool for defining data is the class diagram, which provides a static data model that defines the underlying structure that the data needs to conform to.

Class diagrams are not just limited to defining data. Strictly speaking, a class diagram is a graphical description of the static structure of a system, or some aspect of it, that represents a set of underlying building blocks. Those building blocks could be software components, executable software objects or data containers, such as tables within a database.

While class diagrams have a wide variety of potential uses in the development of digital solutions, this chapter focuses on their use during digital solution definition, to specify the data structures needed to support the required functionality. Therefore, the class diagram is said to provide a static view of data, as opposed to how the data is manipulated or affected over time, which is referred to as a dynamic view. Alternative uses of class diagrams during solution design are considered in *Designing Digital Solutions*.

Classes, objects and systems

Most modern digital solutions are based on **object-oriented** (OO) principles. This means the solution is defined, designed and developed as a set of interacting objects that realise required behaviour (functionality) through the provision and consumption of services. The terminology can be confusing because software components, subsystems, applications and data structures can all be considered objects of differing types and degrees of granularity.

A running digital solution consists of a significant number of objects fulfilling different roles. For example:

- objects such as text fields within a user interface (UI) that allow users to interact with the system and its data;
- objects such as screens (forms) or web pages that are composites of a number of smaller UI objects;
- objects that understand how the flow of certain processes should be performed by the solution and control that flow logic dynamically;
- objects that know how to interact with devices connected to form the solution;
- objects that know how to perform specific platform tasks, such as manipulating a file on a storage device;

- objects that know how to convert streams of data received over a network connection into image files that can be viewed on a computer screen or TV; and

- objects that represent and manipulate real-world business data, such as a customer, an order, a payment, an employee or a training course.

The last bullet describes a kind of business data object, the modelling of which is the subject of this section. Class diagrams can provide a conceptual view of data objects that are independent of any digital solution that is used to store and manipulate the data. When used in this way, they provide a common understanding of the key entities within a business.

When used as part of the definition of a digital solution, class diagrams are often referred to as **analysis class diagrams** to differentiate them from **design class diagrams**. These analysis class diagrams provide a logical view of the data structures required to support the functionality defined in use case diagrams and their associated descriptions. Figure 7.7 shows an analysis class diagram that supports the functionality defined in the use case diagram in Figure 7.5. Note that the ellipses (...) are not part of the UML notation but have been included to indicate that the attribute lists are incomplete.

The main elements within class diagrams are the classes themselves. These are represented as boxes with three compartments. The top compartment contains the name of the class, in the form of a singular noun. Where the name consists of more than one word (e.g. **OrderItem**), the first letter of each word is capitalised and the spaces between the words removed. This is a naming convention widely adopted in the development world, called **UpperCamelCase** or **PascalCase**.

Classes classify different types of object and a key part of the definition of a type of object is the properties (referred to as **attributes** in class diagrams) that define that type of object. The attributes of the type of object being classified are listed in the middle compartment of the class box and are typically named using **lowerCamelCase** (also referred to as just **CamelCase**) convention, where the first letter of the first word is in lower case and the first letter of each subsequent word is in upper case. For example, in Figure 7.7 a **Product** object comprises the attributes **productCode**, **description** and **unitPrice**. This means that each **Product** object will have a specific value for each of these attributes, as shown in Figure 7.8, which shows a specific **Product** object.

Figure 7.8 shows the definition for product P978, where P978 is the product code, which is used as the unique identifier for the object. In the object notation, the object identifier precedes the name of the class in the top compartment, and is separated from the class name with a colon. Additionally, the text in the top compartment is underscored to further differentiate the definition from that of the **Product** class.

The bottom compartment of the class box is used to define a set of **operations** – the actions that can be performed on an object. Operations are typically defined during solution design, and therefore are more relevant to design class diagrams than analysis class diagrams. The use of class diagrams during solution design is explored in *Designing Digital Solutions*.

Figure 7.7 Sales Order Processing system: analysis class diagram

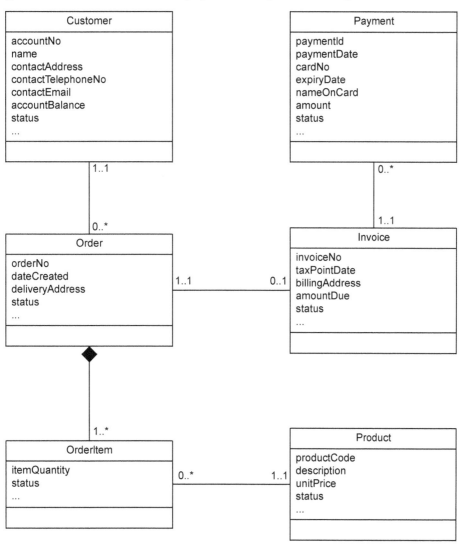

Figure 7.8 Definition of a *Product* object

Associations and multiplicity

The final element in the class diagram in Figure 7.7 is the **association**. Associations represent meaningful relationships between classes and are shown as lines that connect two classes. The nature of the relationship is further defined using two sets of numbers called **multiplicity**. Each multiplicity set defines a range of values (minimum and maximum, separated by two dots) that corresponds to the number of instances of a class – the number of objects. Each association has two sets of multiplicity, one for each of the associated classes. For example, in the relationship between the **Customer** and **Order** classes in Figure 7.7, the multiplicity next to the **Order** class (0..*) denotes that a **Customer** object can be associated with zero or more **Order** objects; the * being a wildcard that indicates that the maximum could be any number; in other words, there is no upper limit. In the same relationship, the multiplicity next to the **Customer** class (1..1) denotes that an **Order** object must be associated with a minimum and a maximum of one **Customer** object. This is often described as 'one and only one', so the relationship between an order and a customer can be described as follows: 'an order is associated with one and only one customer'. Consequently, the multiplicities explicitly describe business rules. Table 7.1 shows the most commonly used multiplicity values with examples taken from Figure 7.7.

Table 7.1 Common multiplicity values

Multiplicity	Example business rule
0..1	An order **may be** associated with zero invoices, but if it is associated with an invoice, it can only be associated with one.
1..1	An invoice **must be** associated with one, and only one, order.
1	An invoice **must be** associated with exactly one order.
0..*	A customer **may be** associated with zero orders, but can be associated with many (unlimited) orders.
1..*	An order **must be** associated with at least one order item, but can be associated with many (unlimited) order items.

Note that where the first number in the multiplicity set is 0 the relationship is optional (denoted by the text 'may be'), but where it is 1 the relationship is mandatory (denoted by the text 'must be').

Composition

In Figure 7.7 the ◆ symbol at the **Order** end of the association with **OrderItem** denotes that there is a special relationship between orders and order items. This relationship is known as a **composition** relationship and denotes that an order is composed of one or more order items. The connection between orders and order items is stronger than a standard association as order items cannot exist independently of their associated order, and if an order is deleted, all of its associated order items must also be deleted. This is referred to as a cascade deletion.

Generalisation

Often when modelling business information or data requirements for digital solutions, the modeller comes across a situation where there are different 'types' of something that share common attributes, but each type may have its own unique attributes as well. For example, further consideration of the class **Customer** in the class diagram in Figure 7.7 reveals that the **accountNo** and **accountBalance** attributes only apply to customers who have registered for a credit account. However, some customers can place an order as a 'guest', and therefore are only required to enter their name and a contact email address or telephone number, for their order confirmation. Additionally, there is a requirement to save details of monthly account statements to account customers only. This scenario can be modelled using the concept of generalisation, as shown in Figure 7.9.

Figure 7.9 Definition of different customer types using generalisation

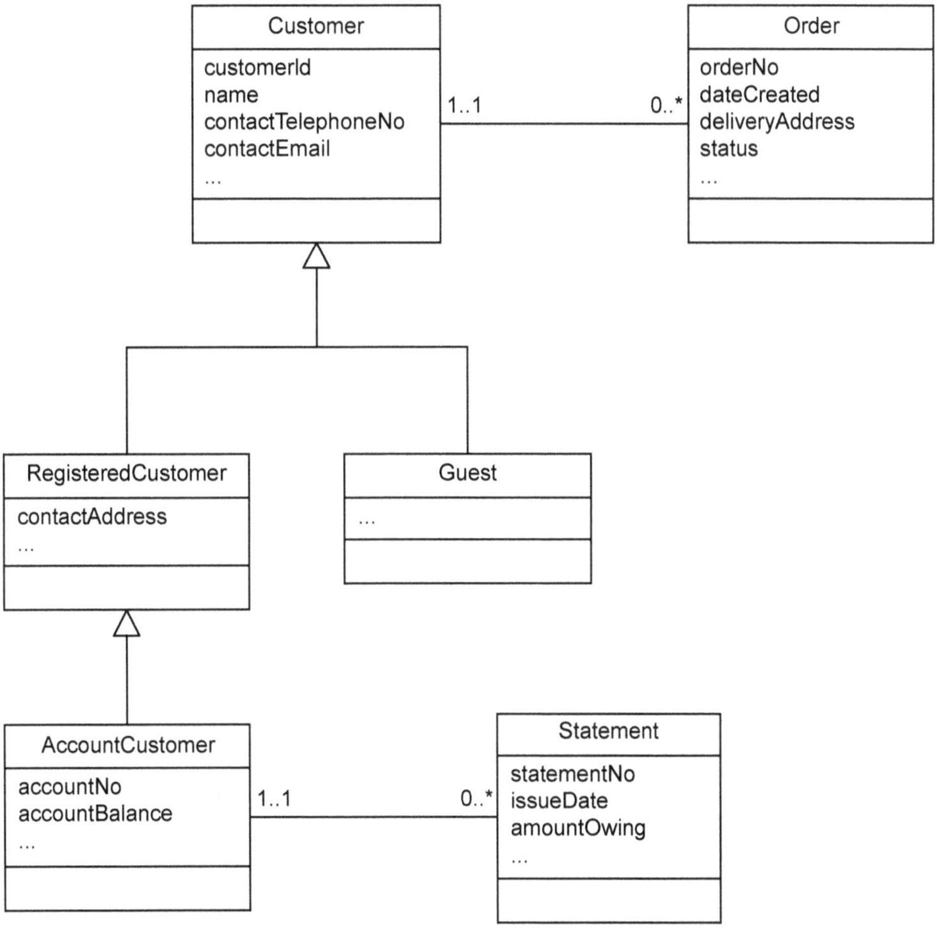

The ⟁ symbol in Figure 7.9 denotes generalisation, so **Customer** is a **generalisation** of the more specific types **RegisteredCustomer** and **Guest**. Similarly, **AccountCustomer** is a more specific type of **RegisteredCustomer**. The generalisation is often referred to as the **super-class** and the more specific types (**specialisations**) as the **sub-classes**. Sub-classes inherit all properties defined for their respective super-class. So, although not explicitly shown in the diagram, the **RegisteredCustomer** and **Guest** sub-classes **inherit** the attributes defined for the **Customer** super-class. So **RegisteredCustomer** and **Guest** objects will have specific values for **customerId**, **name**, **contactTelephoneNo** and **contactEmail**, and **RegisteredCustomer** objects will additionally have a value for **contactAddress**. According to the diagram, **Guest** objects do not have any additional attributes of their own (although as mentioned previously the ellipsis (...) indicates an incomplete list); it is still useful to show it on the diagram as it represents an important concept within the business domain, which may otherwise become lost.

Figure 7.9 actually shows a generalisation hierarchy, which often occurs when modelling. **RegisteredCustomer** is a type of (often referred to as 'a kind of' when interpreting class diagrams showing generalisation) **Customer**, and **AccountCustomer** is in turn a kind of **RegisteredCustomer**. Therefore, **AccountCustomer** objects, in addition to their own specific attributes (**accountNo** and **accountBalance**), inherit attributes from both the **RegisteredCustomer** and **Customer** classes. So each **AccountCustomer** object will have specific values for **customerId**, **name**, **contactTelephoneNo**, **contactEmail**, **contactAddress**, **accountNo** and **accountBalance**.

In addition to inheriting attributes (and operations), sub-classes also inherit associations from super-classes. So, in Figure 7.9, the association between the **Customer** and **Order** classes applies to all types of customer. However, the association between **AccountCustomer** and **Statement** is only applicable to account customers.

MODELLING DYNAMIC BEHAVIOUR

Digital solutions respond to events, which trigger functionality, which in turn manipulates data. The events that trigger specific functionality can be defined as part of a use case description, as shown in Figure 7.4. Use case descriptions can be helpful for modelling system behaviour in terms of the interactions that take place between actors and the system. However, they do not clearly define how the system data is affected by specific events.

State machine diagrams

In UML, the main tool for modelling events and how they affect system data is the state machine diagram,[8] sometimes referred to as just a state machine.

---

8 The state machine/state machine diagram was introduced in UML version 2.0. Prior to this the diagram used for modelling system responses to events was referred to as a 'state chart'. Both state charts and state machines post-date an earlier technique referred to as a state transition diagram.

During the definition of a digital solution, a state machine diagram is typically produced for a specific class from an analysis class diagram, and represents the life cycle of an object of that type (the resultant diagram being referred to as an **object life cycle**). In this context, the state machine diagram shows the various states in which the object can exist, and the changes in state that occur in response to events. During solution design, the subject of the state machine diagram may be a UI (where the states represent screens or pages), or a software component, application or hardware device.

Figure 7.10 shows a state machine diagram that defines the life cycle for an **Order** object. The creation of the object is denoted by the filled circle at the top of the diagram and the destruction of the object by the target symbol at the bottom of the diagram (this notation is the same as is used on an activity diagram – see Figure 7.6). The various states that the object can pass through during its life are denoted with soft-cornered boxes, with a description (typically in the form of an adjective) of the state in the top compartment of the box. The current state of the object at a point in time is recorded in the object's **status** attribute (as can be seen in the **Order** class in Figure 7.7).

The stick arrows show all valid transitions between the states, and the event that triggers a particular transition is annotated on the corresponding line. For example, the event that triggers the creation on an **Order** object is **order placed by customer** and the event that leads to the destruction of an **Order** object is **7 years after archiving**. Note that some transitions also include an additional entry following a forward stroke (/); this denotes an action that takes place and is triggered by the event. For example, at midnight (00:00) following the delivery of the order to the customer, an invoice is raised (denoted by the action /**raise invoice**).

The second compartment of the state box is optional and can be used to record additional actions, typically those that are performed on the object itself. For example, setting the **status** attribute of the object to reflect the new state when the object first enters the state (denoted by the word 'entry' followed by the forward stroke). There are other actions that can be defined within the box, but these are outside the scope of this book.

Interaction diagrams

Interaction diagrams (such as the UML sequence diagram and communication diagram) also show dynamic system behaviour in terms of how the functionality defined in use cases can be realised through interactions between system objects or components. The use of these diagrams to model dynamic system behaviour is typically undertaken during solution design, and is covered in *Designing Digital Solutions*.

Data navigation diagrams

A further technique that can be used to model dynamic behaviour is the data navigation diagram. Introduced in the Information Engineering methodology (Martin and McClure, 1985), data navigation diagrams show how data can be accessed from a logical data structure in order to realise functionality. As this activity is largely associated with data design, data navigation diagrams are covered in *Designing Digital Solutions*.

Figure 7.10 State machine defining the life cycle for an *Order* object

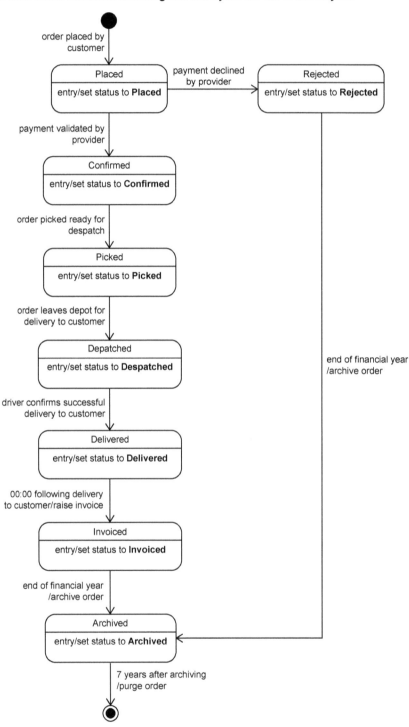

CROSS-REFERENCING MODELS

A valuable by-product of producing different views of a system, as per the three-view approach introduced earlier, is that the different views can be cross-referenced to ensure they are consistent with one another. This offers the following benefits:

- Comparison of the functional view with the data view reveals areas where the data model does not support the proposed processing.

- Comparison of the data view with the functional view discovers areas where processes do not exist to create, modify or delete data items.

- Comparison of the functional view with the event view reveals gaps in the analysis where it is not known in what circumstances (i.e. in response to which events) – and perhaps by who – specific processes are used.

- Comparison of the event view with the functional view shows where there are events that no process has been defined to handle.

- Comparison of the event view with the data view uncovers areas where the data that is needed to handle specific events does not exist.

- Comparison of the data view with the event view reveals where data items have been specified but it is not known in what circumstances these items are created, modified or deleted.

A straightforward mechanism for cross-referencing models is the CRUD matrix. This is a table that lists either events or functionality (use cases) along one axis and data (classes) along the other, and at each intersection (cell) the actions that are being performed upon the data, as follows:

C: One or more objects of the class are being **created**.

R: One or more objects of the class are being **read**.

U: One or more objects of the class are being **updated**.

D: One or more objects of the class are being **deleted**.

Figure 7.11 presents an extended CRUD matrix that shows all three views being cross-referenced using the use case diagram in Figure 7.2 and class diagram in Figure 7.7 as its source.

Standard CRUD matrices either show business events **or** use cases (functionality), but not both. Those based on use cases also do not show the actors associated with the use cases. However, this extended version brings together events, functionality and data to provide a more complete view.

In order to complete the matrix, the modeller requires additional information not shown on the use case diagram or class diagram. This additional information determines which classes are affected by each use case, and in what way, and also which event is

Figure 7.11 Extended CRUD matrix

Event	Use Case	Actor(s) - Primary/ Secondary	Customer	Order	OrderItem	Product	Invoice	Payment
Order placed by customer	Place Order	Customer	R,C	C	C	R		
Order picked ready for despatch	Pick Order	Picker		R,U	R	R		
Order leaves depot for delivery to customer	Despatch Order	Logistics team	R	R,U				
Driver confirms successful delivery to customer	Record Delivery	Driver		R,U				
00:00 following delivery to customer	Raise Invoice	Finance system/Time	R	R			C	

the trigger for each use case. This information can be determined from the use case descriptions.

The entries in the CRUD matrix are straightforward to understand. For example, when the order has been picked ready for despatch (triggering event), the picker (primary actor) invokes the **Pick Order** functionality (use case), which accesses (reads) the required **Order** object and then updates its **status** attribute, in addition to reading the items associated with the order (**OrderItem** objects) and the corresponding **Product** object for each item.

Further inspection of the CRUD matrix in Figure 7.11 reveals the following omissions and inconsistencies, which would need to be addressed by the BA through additional analysis work:

- Although **Customer** details are created as part of the **Place Order** function, there is no functionality to enable these details to be subsequently amended, other than to change the **status** attribute when the order is picked, leaves the depot or delivery is confirmed. Similarly, once created, there is no functionality to amend **OrderItem**, **Product** and **Invoice** details.

- **Product** details are being used as part of the **Place Order** and **Pick Order** functions but there is no functionality to create these details.

- There is no functionality to delete any of the data, which could lead to performance issues after some time, but may also potentially breach legislation (e.g. under data protection legislation, the data subject has a right to be forgotten, and therefore the system would need to provide the ability to delete **Customer** details to comply with this requirement).

- Although **Invoice** details are being created as an automated system process that is triggered at midnight, these details are not subsequently being used.

- There is no functionality to create, read, update or delete **Payment** details.

8 SOFTWARE TOOLS TO SUPPORT DIGITAL SOLUTION DEFINITION

INTRODUCTION

Defining digital solutions requires a suite of software tools, many of which integrate with digital solution design, development and delivery tools. Focusing specifically on tools that support the definition of digital solutions (the first two stages of the life cycle of a digital solution, introduced in Chapter 1), the main tools can be grouped as follows, with some overlap across categories:

- collaboration tools;
- project management tools;
- backlog management tools;
- document management tools;
- business process modelling tools;
- systems modelling tools;
- storyboarding tools;
- prototyping tools;
- wireframe tools;
- CARE tools; and
- CASE tools.

A brief description of each category of tool with a summary of their key features and example products is provided below. Not all tools provide all features of their category and the list of specific tools is not exhaustive.

COLLABORATION TOOLS

Collaboration tools play a vital role in promoting effective teamwork by enabling seamless communication, coordination and idea sharing among team members. Designed to boost productivity and innovation, these tools empower remote and in-office teams to collaborate smoothly and efficiently, ensuring everyone remains informed and aligned.

Typical features provided by collaboration tools include:

- real-time messaging and video conferencing;
- digital whiteboards for brainstorming;
- file sharing and integration with other tools; and
- task tracking and commenting for collaborative work.

Typical examples of collaboration tools include: Microsoft Teams, Slack, Miro, Mural, Google Workspace, Dropbox, Asana and Notion.

PROJECT MANAGEMENT TOOLS

Project management tools enable teams to effectively plan, organise and manage tasks while tracking project progress from inception to completion. These tools enhance workflows, helping teams meet deadlines, evaluate performance and achieve successful project delivery.

Typical features provided by project management tools include:

- task management;
- progress and milestone tracking;
- Agile and Kanban boards;
- resource management and workload balancing;
- Gantt charts, timelines and reporting features; and
- integration with time tracking and communication tools.

Typical examples of project management tools include: Microsoft Project, Monday.com, Wrike, Jira, Trello, ClickUp, Smartsheet, Asana and Basecamp.

BACKLOG MANAGEMENT TOOLS

Backlog management tools support Agile teams in organising, prioritising and refining project backlogs to ensure the smooth delivery of software features or tasks, and focusing teams on high-priority work and maintaining alignment with project goals.

Typical features provided by backlog management tools include:

- Agile and Kanban boards for visualisation and prioritisation of tasks and features;
- backlog refinement and dependency tracking;
- integration with development workflows and tools; and
- iteration planning and burndown charts for monitoring team progress.

Typical examples of backlog management tools include: Jira, Trello, Azure DevOps, Wrike and ClickUp.

DOCUMENT MANAGEMENT TOOLS

Document management tools are essential for centralising, organising and securely managing digital documents. They facilitate efficient document retrieval and collaboration, helping organisations to streamline workflows, maintain compliance and reduce dependence on paper-based processes.

Typical features provided by document management tools include:

- version control and role-based access;
- advanced search and metadata tagging;
- collaboration with commenting and real-time updates; and
- compliance with regulatory standards.

Typical examples of document management tools include: SharePoint, Google Workspace, Box, Alfresco, M-Files, Notion and DocuWare.

BUSINESS PROCESS MODELLING TOOLS

Business process modelling tools empower organisations to visualise, analyse, optimise and automate their workflows and operations. By utilising standards such as Business Process Model and Notation (BPMN), these tools deliver clear process representations that help organisations to identify bottlenecks, enhance efficiency and adapt to changing demands.

Typical features provided by business process modelling tools include:

- support for BPMN standards;
- workflow simulation and validation;
- process automation; and
- collaboration on process design and approval.

Typical examples of business process modelling tools include: Microsoft Visio, Camunda, Lucidchart, Bizagi, ARIS, IBM Blueworks Live and Enterprise Architect (Sparx Systems).

SYSTEMS MODELLING TOOLS

Systems modelling tools support analysts, engineers and architects in analysing, defining and designing complex systems using standardised languages such as UML and SysML. These tools provide a structured framework for visualising system components, interactions and behaviours, ensuring accurate and dependable system specifications.

Typical features provided by systems modelling tools include:

- support for UML, SysML and BPMN;
- simulation and validation of system designs;
- integration with requirements management and software development tools; and
- advanced visualisation for system architecture.

Typical examples of systems modelling tools include: Enterprise Architect (Sparx Systems), MagicDraw, IBM Engineering Systems Design Rhapsody, Microsoft Visio and MATLAB/Simulink.

STORYBOARDING TOOLS

Storyboarding tools help to organise ideas and concepts into sequences of frames or slides to plan visual narratives for projects, designs or presentations. Commonly used in creative industries, UX design and instructional content creation, these tools feature intuitive interfaces and templates that simplify illustrating scenarios, workflows or animations for clear and effective communication.

Typical features provided by storyboarding tools include:

- drag-and-drop interface for creating storyboards;
- pre-designed templates for quick visualisation;
- annotation tools for describing scenes and sequences; and
- collaboration features for team reviews.

Typical examples of storyboarding tools include: Storyboard That, Canva, StoryBoarder and Milanote.

PROTOTYPING TOOLS

Prototyping tools empower analysts, designers and developers to create interactive mock-ups and models of software applications or websites, spanning low to high fidelity. These tools enable teams to test UI flows and refine design concepts before development, conserving time and resources. Their collaborative features facilitate real-time feedback and continuous iteration for optimal results.

Typical features provided by prototyping tools include:

- interactive design elements for user flow testing;
- real-time collaboration and feedback;
- support for clickable prototypes to simulate user experiences; and
- integration with design and development tools.

Typical examples of prototyping tools include: Figma, Adobe XD, Balsamiq, InVision and Axure RP.

WIREFRAME TOOLS

Wireframe tools enable designers to create low-fidelity mock-ups for websites or applications, emphasising structure and layout over visual details. These tools offer predefined UI components to simplify the design process. Wireframes provide a solid foundation for prototyping and development, ensuring user requirements are accurately captured.

Typical features provided by wireframe tools include:

- drag-and-drop elements for wireframe design;
- premade UI components for quick layout creation;
- export options to share with stakeholders; and
- collaboration and version control features.

Typical examples of wireframe tools include: Figma, Adobe XD, Balsamiq, InVision and Axure RP.

CARE TOOLS

Computer-aided requirements engineering (CARE) tools are specialised software solutions designed to support the definition and management of requirements throughout the SDLC by streamlining the processes of eliciting, analysing, specifying, validating and managing requirements. They help BAs to define high-quality requirements that align with stakeholder needs and business objectives, thus enhancing the overall quality of the final product.

Typical features provided by CARE tools include:

- requirements capture and documentation;
- traceability from requirements to implementation and testing;
- change management for requirements updates; and
- visualisation tools for requirements modelling and validation.

Typical examples of CARE tools include: ReQtest, IBM DOORS Next, Helix RM (Perforce), Modern Requirements (for Azure DevOps), Visual Trace Spec and Visure Requirements (Visure Solutions).

CASE TOOLS

Computer-aided software engineering (CASE) tools streamline and automate essential stages of the SDLC. While they were once at the core of development workflows, many CASE tools have since been incorporated into more extensive and specialised software ecosystems. These tools support system design, modelling, code generation and testing, enhancing efficiency and shortening development timelines. Designed to integrate seamlessly into contemporary workflows, CASE tools enable teams to develop high-quality software systems with greater accuracy and reduced error rates.

Typical features provided by CASE tools include:

- support for modelling and design (UML, entity-relationship diagrams);
- code generation (forward engineering) and reverse engineering;
- integration with testing, debugging and deployment tools; and
- workflow automation for development life cycle phases.

Typical examples of CASE tools include: IBM Rational Rose, IBM Engineering Workflow Management (formerly Rational Team Concert), Enterprise Architect, Visual Paradigm, ArgoUML, StarUML, MagicDraw and Modelio.

9 DESIGNING AND DELIVERING DIGITAL SOLUTIONS

Digital solutions have revolutionised our everyday lives. Everything we touch and do these days – ordering products and services, booking our next holiday, reading, listening to music, watching a movie, driving a car, telling the time, calling or messaging a friend, colleague or loved one – will have a digital solution at work somewhere.

This book has provided an in-depth examination of digital solutions, highlighting their transformative impact on our digital society and emphasising their role in addressing business challenges (such as enhancing efficiency and accuracy, lowering costs and driving innovation). In addition to introducing various types of digital solution and encompassing technologies such as artificial intelligence (AI), the Internet of Things (IoT) and cloud computing, it has also considered a range of options for acquiring digital solutions (e.g. bespoke, COTS, component-based and SaaS) and critical methodologies (defined and empirical) for solution development. Key insights have focused on aligning technology with business objectives, leveraging data for decision-making and balancing customisation, cost and scalability.

As well as providing a comprehensive, strategic context for the development or procurement of digital solutions, it has introduced the life cycle of digital solutions, exploring the initial stages (inception and analysis) in detail. The next two books in the collection (*Designing Digital Solutions* and *Delivering Digital Solutions*) continue the journey through this life cycle by taking a comprehensive look at digital solution design, software engineering, software testing and deployment. A sneak preview of *Designing Digital Solutions* is provided here.

Book 2 in the *Digital Solutions Collection* provides a comprehensive guide to digital solution design, structured into nine chapters:

- **Chapter 1** introduces the fundamentals of digital solution design, discussing design objectives and constraints on the scope of digital solution design.

- **Chapter 2** explores different approaches to the design of digital solutions, including monolithic, component-based, service-oriented (including microservices) and domain-driven design. It also covers the distinction between logical and physical design and examines design patterns, notably the Gang of Four patterns.

- **Chapter 3** focuses on input, output and UI design, emphasising the identification of inputs and outputs from requirements through use case diagrams and storyboards. It discusses the selection of input and output technologies and delves into UI design principles, paradigms, techniques such as wireframing and prototyping, user analysis and user journey mapping.

- **Chapter 4** addresses process design, describing key process design constructs (sequence, selection and iteration) and introducing the concepts of stepwise refinement, coupling and cohesion. It provides examples of monolithic and component-based designs, detailing component identification, interaction, interfaces and the design of services.

- **Chapter 5** delves into data design, covering key concepts such as structured, unstructured and semi-structured data, data at rest and in transit, and the distinction between data architecture and data design. It presents data design techniques for online transaction processing (OLTP) and online analytical processing (OLAP) solutions, and looks at special considerations for microservices, mobile apps, IoT and AI applications. Concurrency issues when performing data design and popular data technologies are also explored.

- **Chapter 6** examines cybersecurity and the design of system controls, identifying risks associated with digital solutions, including software failures and cyber threats. It discusses risk mitigation strategies and the design of input, output, data, process, workflow, privacy and security controls, highlighting tools such as encryption, firewalls and AI in cybersecurity.

- **Chapter 7** explores architecture in the context of digital solution design, starting by defining architecture and architecture granularity, and discussing enterprise architecture domains such as business, application, data, infrastructure and security. It explores solution architecture and software architecture, their roles, policies, principles, standards and patterns, including monolithic, client–server, component-based, layered, service-oriented, microservices, event-driven and model view controller (MVC)/model view viewmodel (MVVM) software architecture patterns. The chapter also addresses component and service interactions and introduces Model-Driven Architecture.

- **Chapters 8 and 9** conclude the book with a summary of the range of tools available to support digital solution design and an introduction to book three in the collection (*Delivering Digital Solutions*).

REFERENCES

Beck, K. (1999) *Extreme Programming Explained: Embrace Change.* Boston, MA: Addison-Wesley.

Beck, K., Beedle, M., van Bennekum, A., et al. (2001) *The Agile Manifesto.* Dallas, TX: Agile Alliance.

Boehm, B.W. (1981) *Software Engineering Economics.* Hoboken, NJ: Prentice Hall.

Boehm, B.W. (1986) 'A spiral model of software development and enhancement'. *ACM SIGSOFT Software Engineering Notes*, 11(4). 14–24.

Box, G.E.P. and Draper, N.R. (1987) *Empirical Model-Building and Response Surfaces.* Chichester: Wiley.

Cadle, J. and Paul, D. (2021) *Business Analysis Techniques: 123 Essentials Tools for Success* (3rd edition). Swindon: BCS.

Cockburn, A. (2001) *Writing Effective Use Cases.* Boston, MA: Addison-Wesley.

Cohn, M. (2004) *User Stories Applied for Agile Software Development.* Boston, MA: Addison-Wesley.

Cohn, M. (2005) *Agile Estimating and Planning.* Harlow: Pearson Education.

Covey, S. (2020) *The 7 Habits of Highly Effective People: Revised and Updated* (30th Anniversary Edition). London: Simon & Schuster.

Girvan, L. and Girvan, S. (2022) *Agile from First Principles.* Swindon: BCS.

Girvan, L. and Paul, D. (2024) *Agile and Business Analysis.* Swindon: BCS.

International Institute of Business Analysis (IIBA). (2015) *A Guide to the Business Analysis Body of Knowledge (BABOK® Guide).* Version 3. Pickering, ON: IIBA.

Jeffries, R., Anderson, A. and Hendrickson, C. (2001) *Extreme Programming Installed.* Boston, MA: Addison-Wesley.

Kano, N., Seraku, N., Takahashi, F., et al. (1984). 'Attractive quality and must-be quality'. *The Journal of the Japanese Society for Quality Control*, 14(2). 39–48.

Kotonya, G. and Sommerville, I. (1998) *Requirements Engineering: Processes and Techniques.* Chichester: Wiley.

Martin, J. and McClure, C. (1985) *Diagramming Techniques for Analysts and Programmers.* Hoboken, NJ: Prentice-Hall.

Mellor, S. and Balcer, M.J. (2022) *Executable UML: A Foundation for Model-Driven Architecture.* Boston, MA: Addison-Wesley.

Patton, J. (2014) *User Story Mapping: Discover the Whole Story, Build the Right Product.* Sebastopol, CA: O'Reilly.

Paul, D. (2018) *Defining the role of the business analyst.* Doctoral thesis, Henley Business School, UK.

Paul, D. and Cadle, J. (2020) *Business Analysis* (4th edition). Swindon: BCS.

Poppendieck, M. and Poppendieck, T. (2003) *Lean Software Development: An Agile Toolkit.* Boston, MA: Addison-Wesley.

Ries, E. (2011) *The Lean Startup: How Constant Innovation Creates Radically Successful Businesses.* London: Portfolio Penguin.

Ross, J., Beath, C.M. and Mocker, M. (2019) *Designed for Digital: How to Architect Your Business for Sustained Success.* Cambridge, MA: MIT Press.

Royce, W.W. (1970) 'Managing the development of large software systems'. In: *Proceedings of IEEE WESCON*, Los Angeles, CA, August. 1–9.

Rumbaugh, J., Jacobson, I. and Booch, G. (2005) *The Unified Modeling Language Reference Manual* (2nd edition). Boston, MA: Addison-Wesley.

Scaled Agile, Inc. (2023) *SAFe® 6.0 for lean enterprises.* Available from: scaledagileframework.com

Schwaber, K. and Sutherland, J. (2020) *The Scrum Guide: The definitive guide to Scrum: the rules of the game.* Available from: scrum.org

Tate, M. (2015) *Off-the-Shelf IT Solutions: A Practitioner's Guide to Selection and Procurement.* Swindon: BCS.

Wake, B. (2003) *INVEST in good stories, and SMART tasks.* Blog post. Available from: https://xp123.com/invest-in-good-stories-and-smart-tasks

FURTHER READING

Brennan, K.J., Godwin, S. and Hendrickx, F. (2022) *Digital Product Management*. Swindon: BCS.

Burnett, S. (2024) *AI in Business: Towards the Autonomous Enterprise*. Swindon: BCS.

Evans, N.D. (2017) *Mastering Digital Business: How Powerful Combinations of Disruptive Technologies Are Enabling the Next Wave of Digital Transformation*. Swindon: BCS.

Fowler, M. (2003) *UML Distilled: A Brief Guide to the Standard Object Modeling Language* (3rd edition). Boston, MA: Addison-Wesley.

Fry, H. (2018) *Hello World: How to be Human in the Age of the Machine*. New York: W.W. Norton.

Longbottom, C. (2017) *The Evolution of Cloud Computing: How to Plan for Change*. Swindon: BCS.

Mitchell, M. (2019) *Artificial Intelligence: A Guide for Thinking Humans*. New York: Farrar, Straus and Giroux.

INDEX

Page numbers in italics refer to figures or tables.

CARE (computer-aided requirements engineering)) tools 101, 145, 149

CASE (computer-aided software engineering) 145, 150

change control 40, 79, 92, 98, 99, 101, 110

chatbots 1, 4, 15

class diagram 135, 136, *137*

classes 135, 136, 138, 140, 143

cloud computing 2, 5, 16

cloud solutions 3–4, 15

Cockburn, Alistair 125, 129

Cohn, Mike 68, 71

collaboration 3, 15, 39, 44, 50, 52–4, 64–5, 66, 68, 80, 83, 147–9

collaboration tools 145–6

commercial off-the-shelf (COTS) solutions 29–33, 36, 37, 135

comparison of models 50

component-based solutions 32, 37

composition relationship 138

cone of uncertainty 24–5, *25*

configuration management (CM) 79, 92, 98, 101

content management systems (CMS) 3

context diagram 95, 122, *122*, 123, 124

continuous improvement 5, 53, 59, 65–6. 67. 103

cost of delay 61, 115, 116

critical success factor (CSF) 100

CRM/ERP platforms 32, 33, 36, 37

CRUD (created, read, updated, deleted) matrix 143–4, *144*

customer expectations 16

customer experience 2, 3, 15

customer relationship management (CRM) systems 3, 4, 15, 16, 32, 33, 36, 37

cybersecurity 5, 6

data 1
  analytics 2, 3, 4, 6, 15
  big 5, 6
  breaches 6, 16, 27
  -centric 2
  integration 15
  management 33
  model 94, 95, 135, 143
  modelling 135–40

navigation diagrams 141

ownership 33

protection 6, 16, 86, 144
  requirements 93, 95, 139
  warehousing 6

decision-making 2, 4, 5, 6, 8, 15

decommissioning 9–10

defined approaches (software development) 39–41

definition of done (DoD) 68

definition of ready (DoR) 93

Delivering Digital Solutions 38, 49, 69, 83, 127, 151–2

deployment 9

design 9

Designing Digital Solutions 9, 32, 74, 126, 127, 135, 136, 141, 151–2

development 9, 38–74

DevOps 9

diagnostics 5

digital solutions
  acquiring 29–37
  approach to acquiring 36–7
  benefits 2
  bespoke software development 38–74
  business context 13–28
  business systems and 13–15
  deciding on an approach 50–3
  defined approach 39–41
  defined versus empirical approaches 38–44
  definition 1
  designing and delivering 151–2
  development 19, 21, 22, 23–8
  development life cycle 23
  empirical approaches (software development) 41–4
  investment in 15–19
  key characteristics 2
  life cycle 7–10, *8*
  project changes 110, 112
  software tools 145–50
  types 3–7

digital twins 5

document management tools 145, 147

DSDM (Dynamic Systems Development Method) Agile Project Framework 59–60, 63, 113

ecommerce 3, 5, 15, 16

elicitation techniques 84–5

empirical approaches (software development) 41–4

end-users 34, 40, 42, 44, 66, 69, 82–4, 87, 101, 118

enterprise resource planning (ERP) 4, 15, 32, 33, 36, 37

environmental, social and governance (ESG) 16

extreme programming (XP) 57–60, 63, 66, 68, 89, 106, 107

Extreme Programming Explained: Embrace Change 68

feasibility assessment 21, *22*

feasibility study 23, 46, 47

fixed time development activities 49, 56, 113

flexibility 2, 3, 15, 30, 35, 37, 53, 114

formal review process 91, *92*

forward engineering 127, 150

fraud detection 5

function models 94, 95

functional decomposition 124

functional requirements 9, 78, 82, 84–7, 95, 107, 126

gap analysis 22, 121

General Data Protection Regulation (GDPR) 16

general requirements 86, 87, 107

generalisation 139, *139, 140*

generative AI 4

gherkin scenarios 69–70, *70*, 112

goal levels 125

good requirements 77, 79, 88–9, 92

horizontal traceability 99, *99*

identity and access management (IAM) 6

imperatives 103, 105

inception 7–8, 9, 23, 146

incremental delivery 50, 64, 108, 113, 114

infrastructure as a service (IaaS) 4

initial implementation requirements 103

inspection 42, 43, 93, 144

integrated solution 29